༄༅། །བསྐྱེད་རྫོགས་སུ་ཚོགས་ཀྱི་སྣོར་ཕོར་བུ་རག་རིམ་
འཇའ་ཚོན་གྱི་རི་མོ་བཞུགས་སོ།།

RAINBOW PAINTING

RAINBOW PAINTING

*A Collection of Miscellaneous Aspects of
Development and Completion*

TULKU URGYEN RINPOCHE

Foreword by
CHÖKYI NYIMA RINPOCHE

Translated from the Tibetan by
ERIK PEMA KUNSANG

Compiled by
MARCIA BINDER SCHMIDT
And edited with
KERRY MORAN

RANGJUNG YESHE PUBLICATIONS
Boudhanath, Hong Kong & århus

RANGJUNG YESHE PUBLICATIONS

www.rangjung.com
www.lotustreasure.com

RANGJUNG YESHE PUBLICATIONS
526 Entrada Dr. Apt. 201
Novato, CA 94949 USA

FIRST EDITION 1995

Printed in the United States of America
1 3 5 7 9 8 6 4 2

PUBLICATION DATA:
Tulku Urgyen Rinpoche (1920–1996).
Foreword by Chokyi Nyima Rinpoche.
Translated from the Tibetan by Erik Pema Kunsang (Erik Hein Schmidt).
Compiled by Marcia Binder Schmidt and Edited with Kerry Moran.

Title: *Rainbow Painting, A Collection of Miscellaneous Aspects of Development and Completion*
(Bskyed Rdzogs Sna Tshogs Kyi Skor Thor Bu Rag Rim 'Ja' Tshon Gyi Ri Mo Bzhugs So).

ISBN 978-962-7341-22-2 (pbk.)

1. Mahayana and Vajrayana — Tradition of Pith Instructions.
2. Buddhism — Tibet. I. Title.

Photo of Tulku Urgyen Rinpoche: Jean-Marie Adamini

CONTENTS

"May all goodness, as symbolized by this endeavor, be the cause for all sentient beings to forever embrace the sacred Dharma, and may every one of them, without a single exception, attain the state of liberation."

—*Tulku Urgyen Rinpoche*

FOREWORD

Rainbow Painting contains instructions given by Tulku Urgyen Rinpoche, our lord of refuge and root teacher. Among its contents you will find, in general, the story of how Buddha Shakyamuni appeared in our world and out of boundless compassion imparted the precious Dharma of Statement and Realization to flourish here. In particular, you will find how many learned and accomplished masters established and propagated the Buddhadharma in the snowy land of Tibet. Rinpoche also tells of how countless fortunate practitioners of the past authentically applied the teachings through practice of the three vehicles and gave rise to experience and realization. Undeniably in the past, in India and Tibet, there has been an untold number of learned and accomplished masters.

At present, these complete and unmistaken instructions on view, meditation and conduct — within either the structure of the three vehicles, or, more extensively, the understanding of the nine progressive vehicles — are something we can receive directly through the oral transmission of the lineage masters. The Kangyur and Tengyur, the words of the Buddha and past Indian masters, the collected works of learned and accomplished Tibetan teachers — all these are still accessible to us, in an amount that is uncountable.

Among all these masters, Tulku Urgyen Rinpoche is someone who has lived at length in mountain hermitages, spent many years in retreat, and done a considerable amount of meditation training. For this reason, he gives the very quintessence of the sacred Dharma spoken by our compassionate Buddha Shakyamuni. The extensive Sutra and the profound Tantra, the Mahamudra and the Dzogchen teachings contained in this book extend from the four mind-changings, at the base, up to how to attain the precious state of unexcelled omniscient wisdom, at the top. Rinpoche's advice instructs us in the way we should practice, in a complete and unmistaken manner. We disciples should take the meaning to heart.

The "unexcelled state of unity" is not attained independently of means and knowledge. The common means is proper conduct which is extremely important. Knowledge is the view. In the context of a bodhisattva, the conduct is the six paramitas, while the view is original wakefulness, in which emptiness and compassion are indivisible.

In the context of Tantra, conduct necessitates the understanding that all phenomena included within samsara and nirvana, whatever appears and exists, is the display of purity and equality. The understanding, the knowledge aspect, is that the world and its beings are all-encompassing purity, and that everything is experienced without having any concrete existence. The means is to train in that as the path.

According to the tradition of pith instructions, the ultimate attainment, the unexcelled realization of Samantabhadra, can be pointed out right now in the gap between two thoughts. It is pointed out by a master as nonconceptual wakefulness, the naked state of dharmakaya. Through this pointing-out instruction, we can personally recognize, exactly as it is, the innate state present in ourselves as our nature. By training in this recognition, it can become unbroken and continue throughout day and night.

The teachings of Tantra speak of a certain instruction called "equalizing buddhahood during four periods." This instruction involves resolving the state of nondual awareness during both day and night. It is accomplished to such an extent that the practitioner who is able to continuously release his or her mind into this state of nondual awareness will, in this very life and body, be able to attain the precious and unexcelled state of omniscient enlightenment. The instructions, the key points in how to do this, are available from a master who holds their unbroken lineage. These teachings are right at hand, ready to be requested, ready to be received. I have absolutely no doubt about this. We are so close to receiving such precious teachings and taking them to heart!

We do possess this great fortune. Do not leave the sacred teachings as if it is enough merely to have requested and heard them. Then the Dharma becomes like the old saying: "As the butter skin is never cured by butter, the jaded practitioner is never touched by the Dharma." This is exactly what Gampopa meant when he said, "When not practiced correctly, the Dharma becomes a cause for rebirth in the lower realms!" Why would he say something like that? It is because the failure to sincerely assimilate the words and meaning of the teachings makes us unable to reduce the disturbing emotions present in our stream-of-being. Superficial knowledge of metaphysical words and their meaning cannot prevent our minds being clouded over by the disturbing emotions of conceit and jealousy, competitiveness and ill-will. A person in such a state is a practitioner in name only. Since the real purpose of the Dharma is to soften our rigid character, the benefit will have amounted to nothing. It is for this reason that we should unite view and conduct.

To facilitate this, it is helpful to work at developing further devotion to our root teacher and lineage masters, as well as cultivating compassion for all six classes of sentient beings. It is said in the Vajrayana context: "A time will come when you perceive your master as a buddha in person; a time will come when you have impartial compassion for all beings, indistinguishable from that which you hold for your parents." Experiencing this in an authentic way is the indisputable proof that a person has not only glimpsed and understood the true view, but also to a certain degree has grown accomplished in the authentic natural state.

On the other hand, to regard one's vajra master as an ordinary human being, and to have a love for others that is limited by bias and prejudice, is a sign that we have not arrived at realization of the true view. In fact, it is a sign that we have not even managed to tame our stream-of-being. Be careful! It is for this reason that the practices of accumulating merit and purifying obscurations are so important. The many scriptures of Sutra and Tantra speak of how realization of the ultimate state is facilitated by these practices of accumulating and purifying. The Buddha said in a sutra, "The ultimate state is realized solely through devotion." Therefore, have trust and confidence in our root and lineage masters and in the sacred Dharma, and have compassion for all sentient beings of the six realms. These are not only methods — they are something that is true. It is through this truth that we can benefit ourselves and be of help to other beings. Through devotion and compassion we can realize the ultimate object of realization. We may call this ultimate object of realization Mahamudra, the Great Perfection, or the Middle Way of the Definitive Meaning. It is the natural state of mind, unmistakenly and exactly as it is.

In short, do not separate learning, reflection and meditation training. Rather, try to sincerely assimilate in your hearts what Tulku Urgyen Rinpoche tells us in this book. I feel that this is something of incredibly great importance.

Tashi delek. Sarva mangalam. Gyalgyur chig!

Chökyi Nyima Rinpoche
Ka-Nying Shedrub Ling Monastery
Boudhanath, Nepal

PREFACE

Tulku Urgyen Rinpoche has tirelessly answered questions and offered his unlimited compassionate advice to students who traveled to meet him, from all over the world. *Rainbow Painting* is a compilation of talks given between 1991-1994. These teachings took place at Rinpoche's four main monasteries in Nepal: The Ka-Nying Shedrub Ling Monastery in Boudhanath; Pema Ösel Ling, the monastery surrounding the Asura Cave in Pharping; Ngedön Ösel Ling on a hill top overlooking Swayambhunath; and at Nagi Gompa, his main residence and retreat. The groups varied in size from a few individuals to more than 200 people.

We have presented this book for all sincere Dharma practitioners. It is somewhat a sequel to *Repeating the Words of the Buddha*. We feel that *Repeating* is for students possessing beginners mind to be used as a basis; whereas *Rainbow* is more for the seasoned Dharma student. After consulting with Tulku Urgyen Rinpoche, we selected a range of teachings some of which we hope will benefit those of us who may have become jaded and unenthusiastic. Especially it is an offering to uplift when we fall prey to doubt, misunderstanding and wrong views. Accept the teachings in this book not only to dispel any obstacles on the path but also as an enhancement for practice.

Wherever possible talks have been presented in their entirety. However, some chapters are collected from discourses on the same topic; most were answers to questions; some were a part of seminar lectures. A few followed a different format. The chapter on *The Bardo* was requested and given for our sincere Dharma brother Bill Fortinberry who was suffering from incurable cancer. In the last six months of his life he listened to the tape continuously and in his memory we share it. The chapters on *Samaya* and *Conduct* were a response to counteract the difficulties modern day students undergo; particularly addressing prevalent attitude problems. Finally, the chapter on *Devotion* and *Compassion* was granted as heartfelt advice.

In presenting this book we tried to keep the language as pure, simple and direct as we could; in keeping with Rinpoche's manner of teaching. For explanations of more specific Buddhist terminology, please refer to the glossary in our other books; especially *Advice from the Lotus-Born* and *The Light of Wisdom*. The best way to express the intent of Rinpoche's style is to quote Chökyi Nyima Rinpoche who fully understands it:

"The tradition of Tulku Urgyen Rinpoche and other masters of his caliber is to focus on the simple approach of a meditator, an approach that is saturated with direct, pithy instructions. This is a tradition of plainly and simply stating things as they are, while allowing the student to gain personal experience by alternating questions with advice."

"Tulku Urgyen Rinpoche teaches in a style called "instruction through personal experience." He has spent many years in retreat, practicing in the sense of assimilating the teachings within his experience. Consequently, he speaks from experience, expressing what he himself has undergone. Such teachings are unique, and at times his way of phrasing instructions is amazing. Sometimes they are not particularly eloquent, but always his words have a strongly beneficial impact on the listener's mind. I find that just half an hour of Rinpoche's teachings is more beneficial than reading through volumes of books. That is the effect of instruction through personal experience."

"To teach that the enlightened essence is present within the mind of any sentient being; to teach how this essence is, directly, so it can be recognized within the listener's experience; to show the need for recognizing it and the tremendous benefit of doing so; to show clearly how at that moment the buddha, the awakened state, needs not to be sought for elsewhere but is present within yourself; and that you become enlightened through experiencing what was always present within you — that is what Tulku Urgyen Rinpoche teaches."

In going over the contents of the book with Tulku Urgyen Rinpoche; we asked for a title that he then kindly bestowed. *Rainbow Painting* has come into being with the kind assistance of a few Dharma friends. Special sincere thanks go to them all; in particular to Kerry Moran who perfects Rinpoche's language in its English translation and makes it more accessible. Please forgive any faults as our own and for the benefit of all beings may these teachings be joyfully received.

— *Marcia and Erik Schmidt*

BACKGROUND

THE BUDDHADHARMA WAS TRANSMITTED to the people of Tibet with the patronage of an ancient lineage of kings. It is said that a semi-divine being from the Punjabi royal lineage, who had descended to live among human beings, fled north into the Himalayas. Eventually he emerged from the mountains into the Yarlung region of Tibet. The people of the area mistakenly thought he was a miraculous being who had fallen from the sky, and carried him on their shoulders to establish him as their first monarch. His name was Nyatri Tsenpo.

The first Buddhist scriptures emerged in the Land of Snow after 35 generations of these kings had ruled in an unbroken line from father to son. At that time everyone was illiterate, a fact that filled the reigning king with sorrow. To combat his people's ignorance he prayed fervently. Due to the blessings of the buddhas, three scriptures of the enlightened ones fell from the sky, landing on the roof of his palace. Of course, no one could read them, but the mere presence of these sacred texts transformed the environment so that harvests took place at the appropriate times and the evil forces in the country were somewhat pacified. It was as though the dense darkness of night had been slightly dispelled by the earliest glimmer of dawn.

Five generations later, the great king Songtsen Gampo [617-698 c.e.] took the throne. He invited the first Buddhist teachers to Tibet. Due to his enormous merit, he managed to acquire two of the three main statues located in the main temple in Bodhgaya, the place of the Buddha's enlightenment in India. These two statues were brought to Tibet as the bridal gifts of the two foreign princesses he married. One statue accompanied the daughter of the Chinese emperor, while the second statue was brought by the daughter of the king of Nepal. To continue the analogy, the period of his reign corresponds to the sun just about to rise on the horizon: that is the image for the Dharma beginning its spread throughout the land.

Three or four generations thereafter, King Trisong Deutsen [790-844 C.E.] made a great vow to fully establish Buddhism throughout Tibet; this would be like the sun rising high in the sky. During his reign, he invited 108 great masters to Tibet. In those days, spiritual guides, teachers and masters were called *panditas*. Those who received the teachings and who translated them into Tibetan were called *lotsawas*. The first important master invited to Tibet during this period was the renowned Khenpo Bodhisattva, also known as Shantarakshita.

The king had grand plans to build a group of temples in Central Tibet, the complex that today is known as Samye. Now, Shantarakshita was a great bodhisattva with a tremendously loving and peaceful heart. Because of this he was unable to wrathfully subjugate the local spirits of the area around Samye. A powerful *naga* spirit slandered the bodhisattva, saying, "If these Indians start bringing Buddhism here, it will become difficult for us. Let's all gang up and make trouble." All the eight classes of spirits agreed to try their best to stop Buddhism from spreading in Tibet by preventing the construction of Samye. Whatever was built during the daytime, the gods and demons of the land destroyed during the night. It seemed as though Khenpo Bodhisattva was going to fail in his mission.

The king became very depressed with the lack of progress, so the Khenpo told him, "I'm only a bodhisattva. I can't handle all the powerful spirits of this region, but don't despair, there is a way. In India, at this moment, lives a being who is exceptional in every way; he was not even born from a womb. His name is Padmasambhava, the Lotus-Born. If the local gods and demons who oppose the true teachings simply hear his name, they will immediately be terror-stricken and powerless. Invite him to Tibet, and our problems will end." The king asked, "How can we invite him?" and the Khenpo replied, "We three share a vow from our former lives, when Your Majesty, Padmasambhava and I were brothers who helped erect the great stupa in Boudhanath, Nepal, called Jarung Khashor. Since we vowed at that time to spread Buddhism to the north, Padmasambhava will certainly accept our invitation; we need only request him to come here."

Padmasambhava, who had not been born from a human mother, possessed the tremendous power to subjugate all evil forces. The other great masters chiefly responsible for establishing the Dharma in Tibet were Vimalamitra, an incredibly realized master who attained the vajra body of the great transformation beyond birth and death, and the Tibetan translator Vairochana, an emanation of Buddha Vairochana. Another master named Buddhaguhya also brought Vajrayana teachings. All together, 108 panditas arrived in Tibet.

A great number of Tibetans were educated as translators during this period, so that the entire body of the Buddhist teachings, including various sadhanas and practices, were translated into Tibetan and accurately codified. The temple-complex of Samye was erected with the assistance of Padmasambhava, and the Dharma was fully established throughout the country. The teachings from that period are now known as the *Nyingma* or the Old School of the Early Translations, as opposed to the teachings imported from India during a later period, which are called the *Sarma* or the New Schools of the Later Translations.

A while after the death of King Trisong Deutsen there was a period of religious persecution, in which the evil oppressor Langdarma almost succeeded in eradicating Buddhism. The subsequent revival saw the beginning of the Sarma Schools. These later teachings were chiefly translated by the great translators Rinchen Sangpo and Marpa Lotsawa. These two and other great teachers journeyed to India, received many instructions from the masters there and brought them back to Tibet. All together, eight transmission lineages flourished in Tibet and were later known as the Eight Chariots of the Practice Lineage. One was Nyingma, and seven were Sarma, or New Schools.

Among the New Schools are the Marpa Kagyü, Shangpa Kagyü, and the Lamdrey, this last belonging to the Sakya tradition. There was the Kadampa, which was later reformed into the Gelug school, as well as the Shijey and Chö, which respectively mean Pacifying and Cutting. The Jordruk, or Six Unions, and the Nyendrub or Three Vajra practice of Approach and Accomplishment, likewise appeared. These eight schools were, without a single exception, the teachings of the Buddha. Each taught without any conflict both the Sutra systems, which includes Hinayana and Mahayana, and the system of Tantra, the vajra vehicle of Secret Mantra.

One of the kings of this period, a great religious ruler named King Ralpachen, a grandson of Trisong Deutsen, also invited many masters to Tibet. He had incredibly great respect for practitioners of the Buddha-dharma, placing them even above his head, in a quite literal fashion. Now at that time there were the two assemblages of Sangha, consisting of the congregation of ordained monks, recognized by their shaven heads and Dharma robes, and the congregation of *ngakpas,* or tantrikas, who were distinguished by their long braided hair, white skirts, and striped shawls. As a sign of his deep appreciation for these two congregations, he would spread his two very long braids out upon the ground and allow the revered practitioners to tread on and sit upon his own hair. He would even take pebbles from under their feet and place them on the crown of his head to show respect. The impact of Tibet's king acting as the patron of the Buddhadharma, in conjunction with his great reverence for the teachings, created the circumstances for the Buddhist teachings to firmly take root in and flourish in Tibet.

The other occasion in which perfect conditions occurred in Tibet was during the earlier reign of King Trisong Deutsen. The king himself was an emanation of the great bodhisattva Manjushri, and even some of his ministers were emanations. The masters and panditas invited to Tibet were emanations of buddhas and bodhisattvas, and so were the translators of that time. Due to these incredibly positive circumstances, it was possible for the King to fulfill his vow of establishing Buddhism in Tibet like the sun rising in the sky.

During these two periods, masters and disciples as well as their subsequent disciples attained an incredible degree of realization. Some gurus and students both displayed extraordinary signs of their accomplishment by soaring like flocks of birds through the sky. Wherever they took flight and wherever they landed, they left footprints in solid rock. This is not just a legend from the past; these imprints are visible even today, and you can go and look for yourself.

This was simply a sketch of the origins of the Dharma in Tibet. To sum up, we could say that India is like the father of the Buddhadharma, Nepal is like the mother, and the teachings that arrived in Tibet were like their offspring.

To continue in a more general fashion regarding the Vajrayana teachings: they only arise in a widespread fashion as they do right now during three particular aeons. The first period occurred an incalculable number of aeons before our time, when a buddha named Ngöndzok Gyalpo, the Truly Perfected King, appeared. During his reign Vajrayana was widely and openly propagated. After that until the present age of the truly and perfectly awakened one, Buddha Shakyamuni, the Vajrayana teachings were not fully available. In the distant future will come an age called the Aeon of the Beautiful Flowers, when the Buddha Manjushri will appear and Vajrayana will again be widespread. This does not mean that the Vajrayana teachings will not be taught in the aeons between these periods. But they will be propagated in a fragmented manner, not in the comprehensive and vast way they are available currently.

This present time of the teachings of Buddha Shakyamuni is also called the Age of Strife, or the time in which the five degenerations are rampant, these being the decline — in life-span, era, beings, views, and disturbing emotions. Although people fight amongst each other during this age, the Vajrayana teachings blaze like the flames of a wildfire at this time. Just as the flames of negative emotions flare up, so do the teachings.

There is a saying that plays on the meaning of the names Shakyamuni and Maitreya. "Muni" means capable, while Maitreya means the loving one. The proverb says: "During the Muni, people try to compete with another, while during the Maitreya they will love each other."

During the Age of Strife, it seems as though people are seldom amiable; rather, they are always trying to outdo one another. This fundamental competitiveness has given rise to the name Age of Strife. But this is exactly the reason that Vajrayana is so applicable to the present era. The stronger and more forceful the disturbing emotions are, the greater the potential for recognizing our original wakefulness. In the era of Maitreya, everyone will be loving toward one another, but they will not even hear the word Vajrayana — there will not be any Vajrayana teachings.

It is a fact that at the very moment we are strongly caught up in thought forms or in the surging waves of an emotion, of anger for instance, it is much easier to recognize the naked state of awareness. This of course is not the case when one has trained in a very tranquil, placid state of meditation where there are no thoughts and negative emotions. Then, due to what is called the "soft pleasure," it is actually much more difficult to recognize the true state of nondual mind. Through training solely in serenity we may end up in the Realm of Conceptionless Gods, and remain for aeons in an unbroken state of absorption. This state is similar to being intoxicated with the spiritual pleasure of peace and tranquillity. In fact, however, this repose as a conceptionless god does not help you one iota in approaching the awakened state. Among the traditional eight states in which one is unfree to pursue a spiritual path, taking rebirth among conceptionless gods is the worst circumstance because it is the ultimate sidetrack.

Conversely, experiencing great despair, great fear and intense worry can be a much stronger support for practice. For example, if we are suffering from a fatal illness and we are on the brink of death, if we can remember to look into the nature of mind as we are about to die, our experience will be very unlike the normal training in peacefulness. It is the intensity of emotion that allows for a more acute insight into mind essence.

It is the same when we are really angry, so enraged we feel as though we are one big flame of blazing, focused anger: if we recognize our natural face and just let go, at that moment the state of wakefulness is laid utterly bare, in a much brighter and more vivid fashion than would normally be. Or, if we are suddenly frightened, as when we are pursued by a pack of vicious dogs and the mind becomes petrified, if we can remember, difficult as it may be, to recognize mind essence at that time, the insight will surpass our normal state of insight generated in meditation practice. Thus, the vast amount of conflict in the world today is precisely why the Vajrayana teachings will spread like wildfire.

There are three different approaches to actually applying Vajrayana in practice: taking the ground as path, taking the path as path, and taking the fruition as path. These three approaches can be understood by using the analogy of a gardener or farmer. Taking the ground or cause as path is like tilling soil and sowing seeds. Taking the path as path is like as weeding, watering, fertilizing and coaxing crops forth. Taking the fruition as path is the attitude of simply picking the ripened fruit or the fully bloomed flowers. To do this, to take the complete result, the state of enlightenment itself, as the path, is the approach of Dzogchen. This summarizes the intent of the Great Perfection.

The main teaching of the original teacher Buddha Samantabhadra is Dzogchen, the Great Perfection. The teachings of Dzogchen are the pinnacle of all nine vehicles. Before the Dzogchen teachings arrived in our human world, they were propagated through the *Gyalwa Gong-gyü,* the mind transmission of the victorious ones, in the three divine realms: first in Akanishtha, then in Tushita, and lastly in the Realm of the 33 Gods, the world of Indra and his 32 vassal kings located on the summit of Mount Sumeru.

Akanishtha is of two types: the ultimate Akanishtha, often called the palace of Dharmadhatu, refers to the state of enlightenment of all buddhas. There is also the symbolic Akanishtha, which is the fifth of the Five Pure Abodes and is still within the Realms of Form, located in the sky above Mount Sumeru. The symbolic Akanishtha is the highest among the seventeen worlds in the Realms of Form, situated just below the Formless

Realms. The whole of samsara consists of three realms — the Desire Realms, the Form Realms and the Formless Realms. Above the Desire Realms, seventeen worlds make up the Form Realms. Above them are the Four Formless Realms, also called the *four spheres of infinite perception*. The statement "all buddhas awaken to complete and true enlightenment within the realm of Akanishtha" refers to dharmadhatu, not the symbolic realm of Akanishtha.

To reiterate, after Akanishtha, the teachings were disseminated in the realm of Tushita, another of the Form Realms, where Buddha Maitreya now abides. Then, in the Desire Realms below, the teachings were spread in the realm called the Abode of the 33 Gods. Samantabhadra as Vajradhara taught in Indra's palace, called the Mansion of Complete Victory, on the summit of Mount Sumeru. This was about the three divine realms.

Generally, it is said that the 6,400,000 Dzogchen teachings entered this world via Garab Dorje, the first human *vidyadhara,* who directly received the transmission from the Buddha in the form of Vajrasattva. These teachings first arrived in Uddiyana, and later were propagated in India and Tibet. Before the era of Buddha Shakyamuni the Dzogchen teachings were propagated in our part of the universe by other buddhas known as the Twelve Dzogchen Teachers. Buddha Shakyamuni is usually counted as the fourth guide in this Excellent Aeon in which 1,000 fully enlightened buddhas are to appear in our world. Although in this context he is known as the fourth guide, Shakyamuni is the twelfth in the line of Dzogchen teachers.

No Dzogchen teachings have occurred apart from the appearance of a buddha in this world, so we must count Buddha Shakyamuni as one of the chief teachers through whom the teachings were transmitted. He did, indeed, convey Dzogchen teachings, though not in the conventional manner. His conventional teachings were primarily received by those who had a karmic connection with the teachings appropriate to shravakas, pratyekabuddhas and bodhisattvas. It was not that they were not allowed to receive the Dzogchen teachings; their karmic fortune was such that they received the teachings to which they were suited. The Buddha gave

Dzogchen teachings, as well as other Vajrayana instructions, by first manifesting the mandala of a deity and then imparting the tantric teachings to a retinue seated within that setting. This, however, does not lie within the scope of what was perceived by ordinary people.

The Dzogchen teachings are sealed with three types of secrecy: "primordial secrecy" means they are self-secret; "hidden secrecy" means that the teachings are not evident to everyone; and "concealed secrecy" means that they are deliberately kept secret. All other buddhas also teach Dzogchen, but never in as open a way as during the reign of Buddha Shakyamuni. During this period, even the word "Dzogchen" is world-renowned and can be heard as far as the wind pervades. Despite their widespread nature, the teachings themselves, the pith instructions, are sealed with the stamp of secrecy.

Through his immaculate wisdom, Buddha Shakyamuni always taught after taking into account the abilities of the recipients. In other words, he would not teach at a level above a person's head. He adapted his teachings to what was suitable and appropriate to the listener. Therefore, we can say that those who heard his teachings only assimilated what was comprehensible to someone of their aptitude. Later, when they repeated what Buddha Shakyamuni had taught, their account was according to what they had perceived in their personal experience. But his teachings were not only limited to the personal experience of the receivers, who according to some historical texts were shravakas, pratyekabuddhas or bodhisattvas. The teachings they experienced are contained in the different versions of the Tripitaka, the three collections of Sutra, Vinaya and Abhidharma. The reason that the Buddha did not give the shravakas, pratyekabuddhas and bodhisattvas deeper teachings is because these would not fit into their scope of comprehension. What they received is called the general Sutra system. In addition to delivering these general Sutra teachings, the Buddha Shakyamuni also taught in various locations throughout the universe. Manifesting in the form of a deity as the central figure of innumerable mandalas, he taught the tantras. In this way, we should understand that Buddha Shakyamuni himself, appearing in other forms, was the crucial figure in the transmission of Vajrayana teachings. This is not in the conventional sense, but in the extraordinary sense. So, when we hear that the Dzogchen aspect of Vajrayana was transmitted through Garab Dorje, we should know that it actually came from Buddha Shakyamuni in the form of Vajrasattva. From here it was continued through other masters — first through Garab Dorje, then through various Indian masters and eventually through Padmasambhava and Vimalamitra.

Our main teacher, Buddha Shakyamuni, appointed Padmasambhava as his chief representative to teach Vajrayana. He said that Padmasambhava was the Body-emanation of Buddha Amitabha, the Speech-emanation of Avalokiteshvara and the Mind-emanation of Buddha Shakyamuni himself.

Padmasambhava arrived in this world without a father or mother, appearing in the center of a lotus-blossom. He lived in India for more than a thousand years, and remained in Tibet for 55 years before departing from this world at a pass called Gungtang, the Sky Plain, on the Nepal-Tibet border. Four dakinis appeared to support his horse, and carried him to a pure land known as the Copper-colored Mountain.

Since the time he left Tibet, he has sent a ceaseless stream of emissaries representing him. They are called *tertöns,* or treasure-revealers, and are the reincarnations of his 25 main disciples. Today, we refer to these masters in their various incarnations as the 108 Great Tertöns. Through the centuries they have appeared to reveal the *terma* treasures which Padmasambhava concealed throughout Tibet for the sake of future generations. These termas are discovered in the form of scriptures, instructions, sacred substances, precious gemstones, holy objects and so forth.

Many of these tertöns uncovered what Padmasambhava had hidden in such an impressive fashion that even people who harbored great doubt were forced to admit the validity of termas. Sometimes a tertön would open up a solid rock before a crowd of 400 or 500 people and reveal what had been concealed inside. By openly performing such feats and permitting people to witness the revelations with their own eyes, they completely dispelled all skepticism. Through the ceaseless activity of Padmasambhava this type of tertön has continued to appear right up to the present day. So, the terma teachings come from Padmasambhava himself, and are revealed in an undeniably direct way. This is not some mere legend from long ago: even until recent times, these great tertöns could perform miraculous feats like passing through solid matter and flying through the sky.

The Vajrayana teachings, in particular the Dzogchen teachings that consist of seventeen chief tantras, were bought to Tibet and spread by Padmasambhava and Vimalamitra. While these teachings had been propagated in India by many other masters, their transmission in Tibet is chiefly due to the kindness of Padmasambhava and Vimalamitra. Many centuries later, when Atisha arrived in Tibet, he visited the extensive library at Samye and was amazed. He said "These treasures must be taken from the dakini realms! I have never heard that tantras existed in such numbers anywhere in India." Atisha acknowledged that Vajrayana teachings flourished to a much greater extent in Tibet than they did in India.

Since the time of the introduction of Buddhism into Tibet right up until the present day, a continual revelation has occurred in the form of new terma transmissions. Some of the most renowned are: Longchenpa's *Nyingtig Yabshi*, the *Four Branches of Heart Essence;* Dorje Lingpa's *Tawa Long-yang*, the Vast Expanse of the View; the *Könchok Chidü*, the *Embodiment of the Three Jewels,* revealed by Jatsön Nyingpo; and *Gongpa Sangtal*, the *Unimpeded Realization of Samantabhadra* revealed by Rigdzin Gödem. There have been countless others. A little more than 100 years ago, Jamyang Khyentse Wangpo revealed the *Chetsün Nyingtig*, the *Heart Essence of Chetsün*, while Chokgyur Lingpa revealed the *Künzang Tuktig*, the *Heart Essence of Samantabhadra*. Thus, the Dzogchen lineages are continuously renewed by the discovery of new termas.

One might ask, what is the purpose of heaping up stacks upon stacks of Dzogchen scriptures? There is a very important point involved here: namely, the purity of transmission. As teachings are passed down from one generation to the next, it is possible that some contamination, or damage, of samaya may creep in, diminishing the blessings. To counteract this, Padmashambhava in his immeasurably skillful wisdom and compassion gives us fresh hidden treasures. There is nothing of greater profundity than the Three Sections of Dzogchen: the Mind Section, Space Section and Instruction Section. The distance from the Buddha to the practitioner is very short when a revelation is fresh and direct; there is no damage in the line of transmission. The purity or lack thereof lies not in the teaching itself, but in how distant the line of transmission is. That is why there is a continuous renewal of the transmission of Dzogchen teachings.

The chief disciples of Padmasambhava and Vimalamitra are known as the "king and 25 disciples." They all attained rainbow body, the dissolution of the physical body at death into a state of rainbow light. Such practitioners leave behind only their hair and fingernails. Later on, I will tell a few stories about people who attained rainbow body.

From these practitioners onward, for many, many generations, like the unceasing flow of a river, numerous disciples also left in a rainbow body. Among the three kayas —dharmakaya, sambhogakaya and nirmanakaya — sambhogakaya manifests visually in the form of rainbow light. So, attaining a rainbow body in this lifetime means to be directly awakened in the state of enlightenment of sambhogakaya. A disciple of the great Tibetan translator Vairochana named Pang Mipham Gönpo attained rainbow body. His disciple attained rainbow body, and for the next seven generations, each disciple's disciple in turn left in a rainbow body. In the Kham region of eastern Tibet, there were four great Nyingma monasteries: Katok, Palyül, Shechen and Dzogchen. At Katok Monastery, eight generations of practitioners achieved rainbow body, beginning with its founder and continuing through the succeeding seven generations of disciples. There has been an unceasing occurrence of practitioners departing from this world in the rainbow body up until the present day.

To give a few more examples: about 100 years ago, during the time of Jamyang Khyentse Wangpo, there was a great master named Nyag-la Pema Düdül who accomplished enlightenment in the rainbow form. This was witnessed by 500 of his disciples. Then, right before the Chinese occupied Tibet, another disciple left in a rainbow body. When the Chinese were invading Tibet, there was a nun living in the province of Tsang who departed in rainbow body. I personally heard about this from someone who had been present, and I will relate the story in detail later on in this book. Even after the Chinese occupation, I heard that in the province of Golok, three or four people left this world in the rainbow body. So, this is not just an old tale from the past, but something that has continued to the present day.

THE VIEW & THE NINE VEHICLES

THE VITAL POINT OF THE VIEW in each of the nine vehicles is nothing other than emptiness. Each vehicle attempts to experience this empty nature of things and apply it in practice, in what each maintains is a flawless and correct fashion. No one wants to practice something they know is imperfect. Therefore, each vehicle maintains that its particular view and way to implement it is the genuine and authentic way.

The view, or orientation, of the different vehicles varies accordingly. The view of the Hinayana teachings is to cultivate from the very outset the stillness of *shamatha*. This is perfected by repeatedly placing the attention with mindfulness in a quiet state. Eventually this results in the attainment of total equanimity in the state of stillness where thought has entirely ceased.

From the Hinayana vehicle on up, the concept of what mind actually is becomes increasingly refined and subtle. Yet, throughout all these practices some concept is held on to, even though this concept is more subtle than those involved in our ordinary thoughts.

The shravaka vehicle is usually spoken of as a single approach. Actually, after the Buddha passed away, the shravaka followers divided into 18 schools. One of these 18 sects called *Sarvastavadin* continued in Tibet as a monastic lineage, while another was brought to Shri Lanka and spread into other countries. The other 16 schools have died out. The vehicle for pratyekabuddhas mentions two types of practitioners: the "flock type" like a parrot and the "solitary type" like a rhinoceros.

The vehicle for bodhisattvas, the Mahayana, possesses various approaches, involving the 37 aspects of the path to enlightenment. There are also the different philosophical schools, such as Chittamatra and Madhyamika, known as Mind Only and the Middle Way. Each of these has many subdivisions; it is a very elaborate system of classification. The Madhyamika teachings use intellectual discernment to establish the view of emptiness as being "free from the four extremes and eight mental constructs." The Mahayana practitioner resolves that mind doesn't exist and is not nonexistent, it is not both and not neither. Finally, emptiness is resolved as being beyond the four extremes. This view still retains some subtle notion of or fixation on the idea of emptiness.

Is there any difference in the views of Mahamudra, Dzogchen and Madhyamika? Sometimes, it is said that the ground is Mahamudra, the path is Madhyamika and the fruition is Dzogchen. Whether there is a difference or not depends on what aspect we are discussing. Please understand that Madhyamika is not just Madhyamika; you must define what aspect is under consideration. There are different kinds of Madhyamika, such as the Svatantrika Madhyamika, the Prasangika Madhyamika, and the Great Madhyamika of the Definitive Meaning.

Within the Mahamudra system there is Sutra Mahamudra, Tantra Mahamudra and Essence Mahamudra. Sutra Mahamudra is the same as the Mahayana system describing progressive stages through the five paths and ten bhumis. That definitely differs from Dzogchen, and therefore it is not simply called Mahamudra, but Sutra Mahamudra. Tantra Mahamudra corresponds to Maha Yoga and Anu Yoga in which you utilize the "wisdom of example" to arrive at the "wisdom of meaning." Essence Mahamudra is the same as Dzogchen, except that it doesn't include Tögal. The Great Madhyamika of the Definitive Meaning is no different from the Dzogchen view of Trekchö.

Within the Dzogchen system, there are likewise different levels. It is not enough to say "Dzogchen" without mentioning which particular aspect of it we are talking about. Dzogchen is not a single entity; there are four subdivisions. There is the outer Mind Section, which is like the body.

There is the inner Space Section, which is like the heart, and the secret Instruction Section, which is like the veins within the heart. Finally there is the innermost Unexcelled Section, which is like the life-energy inside the heart, the pure essence of the life-force. What is the difference between these four sections, since all four are Dzogchen? The outer Mind Section of Dzogchen emphasizes the cognizant quality of mind, while the inner Space Section emphasizes its empty quality, and the secret Instruction Section emphasizes the unity of the two. The innermost Unexcelled Section teaches everything — ground, path and fruition, as well as Trekchö and Tögal. This last section is like a person who possesses the five sense-faculties completely intact. Nothing is lacking. Each of these vehicles from the very beginning feels that it is putting the genuine, authentic view into practice, and not a false one. But when viewed from the vehicle above, it appears that the viewpoint of the vehicle below is incomplete; this principle applies all the way up through the eighth yana. Whenever one regards these view from the vantage point of Mahamudra, Dzogchen or the ultimate Madhyamika, these views are all seen to possess subtle concepts.

What is most important concerning the view is to recognize buddha nature. The Sanskrit word for buddha nature is *sugata-garbha*; the Tibetan term is *deshek nyingpo*. We must understand that it is the view we should apply in practice. In the first eight of the nine yanas — the vehicles for shravakas, pratyekabuddhas, and bodhisattvas; the three outer tantras of Kriya, Upa, and Yoga; and Mahayoga and Anu Yoga — progressively deeper notions of buddha nature are kept in mind as the point of reference. In these vehicles the viewer, or observer of buddha nature, is called mindfulness or watchfulness, in the sense of keeping constant guard on buddha nature, like a herdsman keeping watch over his cattle. So in these vehicles there are, then, two things: buddha nature and the constant attention, the "not forgetting" it. Buddha nature should first be recognized, then sustained continuously without any distraction. When watchfulness is distracted from buddha nature, the practitioner is no different from an ordinary person. This is the general principle of the first eight vehicles.

In the Tibetan translation of the word for buddha nature, *deshek* or "buddha" refers to all tathagatas and sugatas, the awakened ones,, while *nyingpo* is the essential nature. Just as the essence of milk is butter, the essence of all the buddhas is the state of realization. This buddha nature is precisely what is practiced in each of the nine vehicles, but exactly how it is put into practice differs, because there is a refinement of understanding that becomes progressively more subtle through the vehicles.

Each vehicle, beginning with the shravaka yana, has its own particular view, meditation and conduct. Each has the same aim, to understand emptiness; and each employs practices called *shamatha* and *vipashyana*. On the Mahayana level, the ultimate shamatha and vipashyana is called the "shamatha and vipashyana that delights the tathagatas." Though the same names are used, their depth is much superior to the shamatha and vipashyana employed in the shravaka system. Every vehicle, beginning with the shravaka yana, practices shamatha and vipashyana, so don't think that at the level of Dzogchen these two are ignored or left out. On the contrary, on the Ati level, the innate stability in *rigpa,* the nondual state of awareness, is the shamatha aspect, while the awake or cognizant quality is the vipashyana aspect. Our basic nature, also called awareness wisdom or cognizant wakefulness, is resolved or recognized through shamatha and vipashyana. To cite a famous statement, "Awakened mind is the unity of shamatha and vipashyana."

The principle we must understand here is stated like this: "Same word, superior meaning." Shamatha and vipashyana are ultimately indivisible. Both are naturally included and practiced in Ati Yoga. The extraordinary shamatha here is to resolve and rest in the true emptiness itself. We do not merely get the idea of emptiness; in actuality, in direct experience, we resolve emptiness and rest naturally in that state. Naturally resting is the genuine shamatha of not creating anything artificial whatsoever, of simply remaining in the experience of emptiness. And vipashyana means not to deviate or depart from that state.

According to ordinary shamatha and vipashyana, shamatha is first cultivated and then vipashyana is pursued. Cultivating shamatha means to produce a state of mental stillness, and then to train in it. Pursuing or seeking the insight of vipashyana means to try to find who the meditator is; trying to identify what it is that remains quiet. It's evident that both of these practices are pretty much involved in conceptual thinking. Only in the Essence Mahamudra and Dzogchen systems is emptiness left without fabrication. In Dzogchen, from the very first, emptiness is resolved without any need to manufacture it. It emphasizes stripping awareness to its naked state, and not clinging to emptiness in any way whatsoever. The true and authentic vipashyana is the empty and cognizant nature of mind.

The special quality of Dzogchen is the view that is totally free from any ideas whatsoever. This view is called the *view of fruition,* meaning it is utterly devoid of any conceptual formulations. Dzogchen is like the highest point of a monastery, the golden top-ornament: above it, there is nothing but sky. The innermost Unexcelled Section of Dzogchen is like the temple's golden top-ornament in that it's the highest point of all the nine vehicles.

When we read a sutra, it begins with the title in Sanskrit; after that comes the body of the sutra. At the conclusion, the scripture says, "The sutra by such-and-such name is hereby completed." In the same way, in Dzogchen all phenomena of samsara and nirvana are completed or perfected in the expanse of the single sphere of dharmakaya awareness. Dzogchen embodies completion or perfection in the sense that *dzog* means "finished" — in other words, there's nothing further; it's done, over with, complete. A quotation from the tantras says: "Complete as one — Everything is complete within awakened mind. Complete as two — All the phenomena of samsara and nirvana are completed."

The Dzogchen teachings are described using the following metaphor. Climbing up a mountain, you can only see in one direction at a time. But once you reach the summit of Mount Sumeru, the king of mountains, you can view the four directions simultaneously; you can see everywhere. The idea is that all the qualities of the lower vehicles are included within the highest view. From the highest view, you can see the imperfections of the lower views, just as you can see everything from the vantage point of the mountain peak. This doesn't mean that the lower vehicles recognize that their particular view is incomplete; on the contrary, each has firm confidence that its particular view, meditation, conduct, and fruition are perfect. Each of the eighteen schools of the shravakas believed their view was flawless. Pratyekabuddhas felt the same, and so on. It is only when we reach the highest point of a mountain that we can clearly see everything below.

That is why the Buddha said about the nine vehicles, "My teachings are a gradual progression from the beginning up to the highest perfection, like the steps on a staircase which extend from the lowest to the highest, or like a newborn infant who slowly grows up."

People are of differing capacity, and are traditionally ranked into categories of higher, medium and lesser capacity. Each of those three categories again has a higher, medium and lower type so that there are nine categories in all. The way of transmitting teachings also differs according to this scheme. For people of the higher, medium and lesser types of the highest capacity, there is the *Gyalwa Gong-gyü,* the mind transmission of the victorious ones, the teachings of Ati Yoga, Anu Yoga and Mahayoga. For the three types of people of medium capacity, there are the three outer tantras of Kriya, Upa and Yoga. For the three types of people of lesser capacity, there are the teachings for shravakas, pratyekabuddhas and bodhisattvas.

It is not that the Buddha's teachings differ in quality so that those we call his "highest" were the best of his teachings while those we call his "lowest" were his worst teachings. All his teachings were excellent. The teachings differ only because people are different. Teachings suitable to a particular mental capacity were given a certain name among the nine vehicles. It is not that the Buddha gave good and bad teachings and that we have to search out the good ones; please understand that it's not like that at all. The teachings were skillfully tailored to the individual person. The Buddha, being omniscient, could perceive the appropriate level of teaching required by whoever came to him and delivered it in whatever way was required. For example, when you give a load to someone, you give them a package that exactly fits their strength. If you give the Hina-yana teachings to a person who has the capacity to understand the Ati Yoga teachings, it is like giving a tiny package to a big strong man who can carry it with his little finger. It is not enough. But if you give the highest Vajrayana teachings to someone of the shravaka disposition, it is like loading a small child with a heavy burden meant for a grown man. The child will fall over and definitely not be able to carry it. Similarly, it is very important that the teachings be given appropriately, according to one's capacity.

As a further categorization, it is said that Maha, Anu and Ati are the three Dharma Wheels of the dharmakaya buddha. Kriya, Upa and Yoga are the three Dharma Wheels expounded by the sambhogakaya buddha. The vehicles for shravakas, pratyekabuddhas and bodhisattvas are the three Dharma Wheels taught by the nirmanakaya buddha. These were transmitted respectively as the *mind transmission of the victorious ones,* the *sign transmission of the knowledge-holders* and the *oral transmission of the great masters.* Yet all were given by the Awakened One, the Buddha — as, respectively, the dharmakaya buddha, sambhogakaya buddha and nirmanakaya buddha.

The teachings are meant to be exactly suited to our own disposition and individual capacity. When we feel that the teaching fits and that it makes sense, we can quickly progress training ourselves in it. For example, when a bodhisattva type of person receives the Mahayana teachings, he can quickly progress through those teachings.

When people first come into contact with Tibetan Buddhism, they might think, "What a strange religion! Tibetan Buddhism is full of different forms of deities and rituals — how odd!" The way individuals are raised in other Buddhist traditions can be a bit limited. Due to not being well-educated in a wider approach they believe that their form of Buddhism alone is Buddhism, and what exists elsewhere is not. This attitude is like a person who possesses only one arm, or one leg, or only a head, or the entrails of a human body, while missing the rest of the components: he is not a complete human being. Such a narrow viewpoint is only because of not being well educated. A great scholar or someone who is well-versed in the entire body of the Buddhist teachings will not have this problem at all. He will be able to see where everything fits. He will not fall into the limited situation of thinking, "What's the use of Mahayana or Vajrayana. The shravaka teachings are sufficient. Why can't everyone simply practice that; all the other teachings don't matter." Others may think, "Mahayana teachings are the real thing; the other teachings don't really count." Still others say, "Vajrayana is correct, what is the use of lower teachings, such as Mahayana or Hinayana?" All of these attitudes are complete nonsense. We need to have a complete human body to function.

For example, to build a perfect temple, it must first have solid ground and a proper foundation for it to rest upon. These two elements are the Hinayana teachings. Without a foundation, there is nothing to build on. Second, you need a large and beautiful structure: this is like the Mahayana teachings. Finally, it should not be an empty house, but should possess exquisite representations of enlightened body, speech and mind. These are like the Vajrayana teachings. Otherwise, it is like any other worldly palace — not of real benefit. Similarly, we should combine and unify all three levels of teachings into a single body of practice. Our practice then becomes like a perfect temple, possessing a proper foundation, a magnificent structure, and the representations of enlightened body, speech and mind inside. This is the way to unify the Hinayana, Mahayana and Vajrayana levels of teachings within one single system.

The most important aspect of this unification is the correct viewpoint. It is our job to find out exactly what orientation or perspective can truly put an end to ignorance and confusion. What perspective is genuine and what perspective is false? It is up to us to settle this thoroughly. This does not mean we have to study all the innumerable details, like a great pandita, because our life is not long enough to do that. We would run out of years. Instead, focus on the tradition of the pith instructions, which states the most essential point like this: "Resolve the nature of your mind; don't resolve the characteristics of all the teachings."

The tradition of pith instructions is very important. It is a system of few words which condense the essential practice to its vital points. Through the oral traditions of the Middle Way, Mahamudra, Dzogchen and also of the system known as *Prajnaparamita,* transcendent knowledge, we can personally apply these pith instructions and meet face to face the buddha nature that is present in ourselves.

The difference in the levels of practice depends on the degree to which conceptual mind is involved. The differences between the vehicles are not marked by using the same terminology but by the use of progressively superior levels of meaning. As I mentioned before, when examined from above, the lower yanas appear to have a slight fault because a conceptual frame of mind is still present. That which propels us endlessly through samsara is dualistic thinking. It is said that the first eight vehicles are still the domain of conceptual mind, although this conceptuality does become increasingly subtle. The difference between them and Dzogchen, Mahamudra and Madhyamika is that the ultimate view is free of conceptual mind, unlike in the first eight vehicles. As long as there is conceptual mind, the view is not ultimate. The ultimate view is free of fixation. We cannot become enlightened by conceptual mind; this point is accepted in all the different schools. The Sakya school has a quotation: "If fixation is present, you do not have the view." The Geluk school as well understands that the highest view is free from conceptual mind. What it all comes down to is simply how the task of dissolving conceptual mind is approached.

The difference between the vehicles lies exclusively in how gross or subtle our conceptual understanding is. All the way up to the eighth vehicle of Anu Yoga there is still some conceptual frame of mind. Only the view of Dzogchen or Essence Mahamudra is totally free from conceptual mind. For this reason, it is said that the other vehicles take a very long time to carry one to enlightenment. The shravaka teachings take incalculable aeons. The bodhisattva vehicle takes such an incredible number of lifetimes that they are almost impossible to count. The three outer tantras of Kriya, Upa and Yoga take sixteen or thirteen lifetimes to reach fruition. According to Dzogchen or Mahamudra, when nondual awareness has been genuinely pointed out and correctly recognized, it is like the flawless dharmakaya placed directly in the palm of your hand. Try to apply the correct view in practice, from the moment of waking up throughout the whole day and most of the night, except for three hours of sleep. Then you will not need more than thirteen years to attain complete enlightenment!

Enlightenment is possible when a qualified master meets a worthy, receptive disciple who possesses the highest capacity, and transmits, or points out, the unmistaken essence of mind so that it is recognized. It can indeed be pointed out; it can indeed be recognized; and it can indeed be trained in. If the student practices this for thirteen years, he or she can unquestionably attain complete enlightenment. So another difference between the vehicles is the amount of time it takes to reach complete enlightenment.

From the viewpoint of the highest vehicle, all the vehicles below are like someone who is talking about the moon but has never actually seen it. He may describe how it looks, what it is made of, how it waxes and wanes and so forth, but it is all hearsay. To point out a subtle distinction, this analogy can be connected with the gradual approach of the Mahamudra system wherein one progresses through the path by means of four yogas. The first yoga of *one-pointedness* is shamatha. The second yoga of *simplicity* is vipashyana. At the beginning of simplicity comes a point when the practitioner is like a person who, on the third day of the lunar calendar, is told, "Look up into the sky." The student looks up and sees the sliver of moon. Although it is just a sliver, it is indeed the moon. This is called the moment of recognizing mind essence. One truly experiences emptiness for the first time. Once the nature of mind has been pointed out, it is seen directly without any fault or error. The moon will grow fuller and fuller from the third to the fifteenth day. In the same way, one grows more and more used to mind nature so that it becomes uninterrupted. There is no realization beyond this unbroken recognition of buddha nature. However, before actually seeing the moon we can only talk about it, draw a diagram of it and look at that. This is all conceptual understanding. The real moon is seen for the first time when we are introduced to the view.

THE THREE VAJRAS

Now I would like to explain three pieces of advice given by Atisha, called the Three Vajras. For a very, very, very long time, we have been roaming throughout samsaric existence from one life to the next. We have died and been reborn and died again, almost endlessly. It is as if we are moving through a huge ocean. The Buddha said, "Samsaric existence is like an endless ocean of sorrow." Notice he did not say it was an ocean of bliss and happiness: samsara is always called the "ocean of suffering," never the "ocean of bliss."

If we acknowledge this fact and have faith in it, if we truly desire to be free from this suffering, who can make us free? It's not the ruler of the country we inhabit, nor our father or mother, our friends, our servants, our fame, or our wealth — none of this can free us from deluded samsaric existence. Only the spiritual endeavors we personally engage in can do so. Once we understand this, we should not let ourselves be dissuaded or falter from that path. So the first advice from Atisha is "Place before you the unshakable vajra of no dissuasion."

To place before you the vajra of no dissuasion means: do not let anyone — no matter who they are, not even your spiritual teacher — discourage you from practicing the Dharma. A true master who wants you to be free will never say, "Do not pursue the Dharma." So, the very first step on the spiritual path is to form the unshakable attitude, "I will let no one and nothing dissuade me from practicing the Dharma." If your teacher tells you, "Do not follow your spiritual inclination," you have probably made a mistake in choosing that guru.

Similarly, do not let anyone bribe or threaten you to make you not engage in spirituality. Someone may say, "I will offer you half the wealth of this world if you promise not to practice the Dharma any more. Just give up spirituality, and I furnish the money." We should not let this kind of inducement tempt us. On the other hand, someone might threaten you, pointing a gun at your chest and say, "I will pull the trigger unless you promise to abandon all religious endeavors!" With your mouth, you should of course say, "Yes, I will give it up," but from inside, from the core of your heart, you most definitely should not agree.

There is a less dramatic and more immediately practical application of this point, which is the reason I bring this up. We often hear the saying, "appearances are seductive, and mind is fickle." Beguiling appearances means that when we see beautiful forms, hear pleasant sounds, smell sweet fragrances, eat delicious food, and feel soft textures touching our body, our mind is immediately attracted. These pleasant objects capture our attention and hold it. On the other hand, when we encounter what is unpleasant — ugly forms, harsh sounds, foul odors, disgusting tastes and rough textures —we feel repelled, maybe even aggressive. Dualistic mind is fundamentally unstable in this respect. The type of attention that is easily captivated or turned off is inherently unsteady. When this normal, unstable and fickle state of mind meets with an enticing phenomenon, it gets carried away. To avoid being constantly carried away, we need to make a firm, unshakable resolve. This is the first of the three points: lord Atisha tells us to make a firm decision, to "place before you the vajra of no dissuasion."

The second of the Three Vajras is, "Place behind you the vajra of no shame." When we first take up Dharma practice, we feel a strong wish to be free. We want to renounce further involvement in samsaric states through spirituality. Yet there is a common saying in Tibet: "The new meditator gives away gold, while the old meditator hoards his worn-out shoe soles." In other words, in the beginning we have the feeling that nothing in this world really matters; we can easily give it all away, thinking, "I am not attached to anything!" Then slowly, two or three years later, we start to become jaded and numb. Even useless old shoe soles take on a new importance. Perhaps we think, "These can be cut up and used as tethers to tie the yaks together." We start holding on to things, planing all sorts of later uses for them.

To place the vajra of no shame behind you concerns as well the impression we make on ourselves and other people. For example, when people know that an individual has stepped onto the spiritual path, there is an accompanying responsibility. If later on he or she turns back and gives it up, that action destroys the pure perception in others and may even ruin the Dharma for them. Thus, it is better to begin slowly and progress gradually on the path than to start out brilliantly and later become jaded and insensitive.

We should be like a mountain deer who has caught its foot in a trap. When it manages to yank its foot loose it will one-pointedly dart off to an unpeopled place. It is best that we adopt this kind of attitude. Then, in this very body and lifetime, we can abandon all attachment to our homeland and personal links. Living in unknown places, we can be like a child of the mountains. In this way, both ourselves and others will benefit. Others will see that the teachings work, and will gain the assurance that practice makes it possible to leave behind samsara in this very life and attain some accomplishment. Therefore, it is important to make up our mind at the outset, placing behind ourselves the vajra of no shame. Then later on we will not feel any regret for what we have done.

The third vajra is "Keep company with the vajra of pure wisdom." Here, the purity of wisdom referred to is that of original wakefulness. This is our buddha nature, the enlightened essence, also called *rangjung yeshe,* self-existing wakefulness. We should first recognize this, decide upon it and gain confidence in our ability to liberate all thought states. After recognizing, we train in the strength of that recognition, until finally we attain stability. Making the decision to do so is the third vajra — "Keep company with the vajra of pure wisdom." The "vajra of pure wisdom" is the self-existing wakefulness that is always with us because it is our nature. To form the resolve, "I will recognize my own nature as it is!" is the last of the Three Vajras.

There is another series of Atisha's sayings called the "Four Aims." The first is "Aim your mind at the Dharma." That means your final aim should be directed at what is true and meaningful rather than at mundane attainment. When we direct our aim toward the Dharma, we can attain liberation and enlightenment; but if we aim at mundane achievements, there is no way in the world we can reach liberation or enlightenment.

Atisha also said, "Aim your Dharma practice at simple living," not great wealth. It is easier to pursue the teachings if we are simple practitioners. If we have accumulated great wealth before we begin to practice the Dharma, we feel we have to maintain a certain standard of living. It requires incredible effort to increase our wealth, to guard our assets, to make sure they are not depleted. There is much worry and involvement in that; so, it's best to aim your practice at living simply.

The third aim is "Aim at simple living for your entire life," not just for a short while. Do not think, "All right, I will practice Dharma as a simple practitioner for a little while and then later on I will make a breakthrough and become rich and important." Do not think this way. Instead, aim at remaining a simple practitioner for your entire life, until the time of death.

Finally, Atisha said, "Aim your death at solitude." This means decide to die alone and friendless in a retreat hermitage or unpeopled place, without being surrounded by attendants and companions. These were the "Four Aims."

Atisha also told us to "keep a low seat," meaning a low profile. Don't strive to be high and important. Wear simple clothing, not fancy expensive garments; wear whatever you come by. Moreover, he said, "Let food, clothing and reputation take the defeat." For example, when a dispute is settled, one party wins while another loses. Let food, clothing and reputation "lose the case." In other words, do not let your mind become preoccupied with food, clothing, fame and importance.

Atisha moreover said, "Be your own teacher." Be your own guide. Do not remain in a situation where you must always take orders from others.

Live in a way that allows you to rely on yourself. If you can live like this, you have the possibility of being a pure practitioner."

The great master Atisha himself lived by these principles, and achieved great accomplishment. We should try our best to apply as much as we can of his advice.

Once you decide to practice the Dharma, carry it through to the end. Otherwise, it is as Paltrül Rinpoche said: "When young, we are controlled by others and cannot practice." Usually, until people are about 17 or 18 years of age, they must take orders from their parents or remain stuck in school or at home; they cannot just walk off and practice. Paltrül Rinpoche's quote continues, "In adulthood, we chase after the objects of pleasure and cannot practice. When we are old, we lose our physical strength and cannot practice. Alas, Alas! What do we do now?"

So, if we want to practice, we should make up our minds how to do so. It's best if we can be perfect, pure, whole-hearted practitioners. If not, at least try to embody half of what has just been mentioned, or at the very least take to heart a single piece of this advice and truly live it.

The Buddha treated all sentient beings as considerately as he would have his own parents or children. When he spoke and gave others advice, he did so as sincerely as a father or mother, lying on their deathbed, would give final words to a son or daughter. In this sense, all the teachings of the Buddha are words spoken from the heart, like the final words of advice from a dying parent.

When we apply the teachings of the Buddha, we carry them out in three steps or stages. At first, we study the teachings, learning them thoroughly. Second, we reflect upon them, trying to clearly understand. Third, we train in them, bringing what has been taught into our experience. There should be some effect from this. Studying the Buddha's teachings means we learn about good and evil actions. We understand our choices. We comprehend that everything is created by karmic deeds and our own disturbing emotions, and we discover how to purify and eliminate these. By learning this, reflecting upon it and finally applying it, there should be some outcome, some result. It is said that the result of learning and reflection is that one becomes gentle and disciplined. The result of meditation training is that disturbing emotions like aggression, attachment and dullness steadily decrease. This is the real sign of meditation practice.

THE VITAL POINT

As I mentioned in the first chapter, before the Dzogchen teachings appeared in this world, they spread in the three divine realms called Akanishtha, Tushita and the Abode of the 33 Gods on the summit of Mount Sumeru. Akanishtha, in this case, the symbolic Akanishtha is where Dzogchen was taught to the gods, and it is within samsara. This is as opposed to the ultimate Akanishtha, which is the realm of the buddha nature itself. In this symbolic Akanishtha, the dharmakaya buddha Samantabhadra manifested out of the spontaneous sound of dharmata and taught the Dzogchen tantras.

The teachers of the three kayas, in the context of Ati, are called the dharmakaya buddha Samantabhadra, the sambhogakaya buddha Vajradhara, and the nirmanakaya buddha Vajrasattva. Vajrasattva was the buddha who transmitted the Dzogchen teachings to the first human *vidyadhara,* the knowledge-holder Garab Dorje. It is said he received the six million four hundred thousand Dzogchen tantras directly from Vajrasattva.

Buddha Shakyamuni was the last of the twelve holders of the Dzogchen teachings. But the person who actually spread them in this world was the human vidyadhara, Garab Dorje. How was it transmitted? Vajradhara is said to be the manifestation of the dharmakaya buddha, Samantabhadra, yet with all the adornments. He is the same buddha, but when he appears in a form that is fully ornamented he is known as Vajradhara. At the same time, Vajradhara, in his sambhogakaya buddha form, transmitted Dzogchen teachings. His emanation is Buddha Vajrasattva, who passed on the Dzogchen teachings to Garab Dorje. Garab Dorje is the first human being who disseminated these teachings, but as I mentioned earlier, that does not mean that Buddha Shakyamuni was not a holder of those teachings. Still, the one who truly propagated the 6,400,000 verses, or *shlokas*, of the Dzogchen tantras in our world was Garab Dorje. He condensed them all into three sentences called the *Three Words That Strike the Vital Point* — recognize your own nature, decide on one point, and gain confidence in liberation.

Within Ati Yoga are subdivisions such as the outer Mind Section, the inner Space Section and the secret Instruction Section. The fourth subdivision, called the innermost Unexcelled Section or sometimes the innermost Heart Essence, consists of the extraordinary Dzogchen teachings. It is said that the ultimate view of the teachings given by the nirmanakaya buddha is the view of the Middle Way, Madhyamika. The ultimate view given by the sambhogakaya buddha is Mahamudra. The ultimate view given by the dharmakaya buddha is Dzogchen, the Great Perfection. Although Buddha Shakyamuni had, of course, realized the nature of all nine vehicles, in his function as a nirmanakaya buddha he publicly gave teachings appropriate for shravakas, pratyekabuddhas and bodhisattvas. The primary view, in this case, was the Middle Way, Madhyamika. Garab Dorje emphasized Ati Yoga, especially the Dzogchen view of the outer, inner and innermost sections of Mind, Space and Instruction. He condensed all the Dzogchen tantras into the three statements previously mentioned.

The first of these three statements instructs you to "Recognize your own nature" — buddha nature itself, which is "empty cognizance suffused with awareness." This nature is empty in essence yet naturally cognizant. These two aspects are indivisible, and this unity is also called unconfined capacity. Recognizing your own nature for what it is, is the first of the three words of Garab Dorje.

Buddha nature, itself, is the very basis or source from which all worlds and living beings originate. Whatever appears and exists comes from it. How do we describe buddha nature? It is empty in essence and cognizant by nature, and its capacity is "suffused with self-existing awareness." This is the universal ground from which everything arises. We should understand that it does not fall into any category, such as an entity that

48

exists or does not exist. The claim that buddha nature is a "thing" that exists, is incorrect. It is not a concrete thing with distinguishable characteristics; instead, it is wide open and indefinable, like space. However, you cannot claim that it is nonexistent, that there *is not* any buddha nature, because this nature is the very basis or source of everything that appears and exists. So buddha nature does not fall into any category such as being or not being. Neither does it fit into the category called "beyond being and not being:" it is beyond that formulation, as well.

Buddha nature is said to resemble space. Can we say that space exits? Can we say that it doesn't? We cannot, because space itself does not comply with any such ideas. Concepts made about space are merely concepts. Space, in itself, is beyond any ideas we can hold about it. Buddha nature is like this. If you say that space exists, can you define it as a concrete existent entity? But to say there is no space is incorrect, because space is what accommodates everything — the world and beings. And if we think space is that which is beyond being and not being, that is not really space, it is just our concept of it. So, the first point of Garab Dorje's is to recognize our own nature and to acknowledge how this nature is, not as our conceptual version of it but in actuality.

This buddha nature of ours, which is primordially free from the two extremes of being and not being, is described with the word "unity." What does unity mean in this context? Right now, visual forms, sounds and smells and so on are all present in our experience. If buddha nature were nonexistent, there could be no such experiences taking place. But if we say buddha nature does exist, then what is it that experiences? Can you pinpoint it? You can't, because it's empty of all identity, right? Thus, there is no confining these two — perceiving and being empty. While perceiving, buddha nature is empty of a perceiver; while being empty, there is still experience. Search for the perceiver; there is no "thing" to find. There is no barrier between the two. If it were one or the other there should either be a concrete perceiver who always remains, or an absolute void. Instead, at the same time vivid perception takes place, that which perceives is totally empty. This is called the unity of experience and emptiness, or the unity of awareness and emptiness. The fact of experience eliminates the extreme of nothingness, while the fact that it is empty eliminates the extreme of concrete existence.

In this way, we can say that existence and nonexistence are a unity. This unity is not something we can devise intellectually, which is why it is called the "view beyond concepts." We hear the view described as *thatness* — "just that," simply as it is. Buddha nature is not identical to space, which is incapable of perception. Don't we agree that there is experience? This basis for experience is the cognizant quality. Can these two aspects — empty in essence and cognizant by nature — be separated? If not, that means they are a unity. This unity is what we should recognize when recognizing our buddha nature. To see this fact is what Garab Dorje meant when he said "recognize your own nature."

Garab Dorje's second statement is "Decide on one point." The empty essence is dharmakaya while the cognizant nature is sambhogakaya. The unity of this, the all-pervasive or unconfined capacity, is nirmanakaya. Once we recognize our buddha nature, we should then decide on one point, meaning that the three kayas of all the buddhas is present simply in that. "To decide on one point," means to resolve the state free from ignorance and deluded thought. We recognize directly the fact of emptiness; we realize that our nature cannot be pinpointed. The fact of knowing that it is not something to pinpoint proves the cognizant quality. We cannot separate these two aspects — emptiness and cognizance — because they are a unity. In this way, they are the identity of the three kayas. There is nothing higher or superior to this to decide upon.

Garab Dorje's third statement is "Gain confidence in liberation." It is said that meditation is not the most important thing; liberation is. Mere meditation, such as the state of stillness in shamatha meditation, is not necessarily a liberated state. It is not enough to be concentrated while remaining deluded, because training in such a state only leads to rebirth in the *dhyana realms*. The Buddha proved definitively that mere meditative concentration is not sufficient to gain liberation. Through meditation alone, one ends up in the realms of the meditation gods and the Formless

Realms, states which in themselves definitely do not lead out of samsara. There is a famous quote: "If you know how to meditate, but not how to be free, then aren't you just like the meditation gods?" So, it's very important to know how to liberate your deluded thinking. That is the vital point.

Liberation of thoughts can be described as occurring in several different ways. The great master Vimalamitra mentioned three types of liberation. His description can be applied either to the progress of a particular individual or to the different types of capacities of individuals. The first example is said to be like meeting someone you already know; the second is similar to a knot tied in a snake, and the third is the analogy of a thief entering an empty house.

Recognize the thought as it occurs so that it is liberated simultaneously with its arising. This is very much unlike the stream of thoughts that surges through the mind of an ordinary person. Often called "black diffusion," this state is an unwholesome pattern of dissipation in which there is no knowledge whatsoever about who is thinking, where the thought comes from, and where the thought disappears. One has not even caught the "scent" of awareness; there are only unwholesome thought patterns operating, so that one is totally and mindlessly carried away by one thought after another. That is definitely not the path of liberation!

In the beginning, if we have already recognized our nature even once, we have caught the scent of it. Once you get a "whiff" of your nature, it becomes familiar, like someone you already know: you do not need to doubt who your friend is when you meet him. At this point, thoughts are liberated upon recognition, like the vanishing of a drawing on water.

We can grow more and more accustomed to this fact through practice. Once the practitioner gains an immediate recognition of buddha nature, there is no need to apply any additional technique at all. The same moment a thought starts to move; the thought is liberated by itself. It is like a knot tied in a snake that does not have to be untied by anyone because it unravels by itself. This exemplifies becoming more stable in the training.

Finally, the third analogy of the liberation of thoughts is described as being like a thief entering an empty house. This is called stability or perfection in training. A thief entering an empty house does not gain anything, and the house does not lose anything. All thought activity is naturally liberated without any harm or benefit whatsoever. That is the meaning of gaining confidence in liberation.

There is also what is called the four modes of liberation: self-liberated, liberated upon arising, directly liberated and primordially liberated. These are not exactly a direct sequence, but are more like different aspects or modes of how liberation is. For example, the fourth one, which is primordially free, refers to the awakened state of *rigpa* that is already free; it does not have to be liberated. That's the idea. One of the lines in the *Tsigsum Nedek*, the *Three Words to Strike the Vital Point*, says: "By recognizing dharmakaya in what is liberated, as in the analogy of drawing on water, there is unceasing self-occurring self-liberation."

"Primordially freed" means a state which does not have to be re-freed, because it is already free. With "directly freed', "directly" has the connotation of immediacy, meaning instantaneously. "Naturally freed" is without an entity that needs to be freed; there is no thing or essence or identity that needs to be liberated. Seeing this, it is naturally freed. "Self-freed" means without even the need for a remedy. "Freed upon arising" refers to thoughts that dissolve the moment you recognize the awakened state.

Sometimes five ways of liberation are mentioned. The additional one, *ta-dröl*, "universally freed," means no matter what kind of expression or state occurs, they are all freed in the same way, thus "universally freed." In other words, it does not matter which emotion or thought takes place; all are freed by recognizing rigpa. "Universally freed" means that everything is freed; it is not that only one type of emotion is liberated upon arising while the others are not. All the 84,000 types of disturbing emotions are liberated immediately in a single moment without the slightest remainder. We could view these different types of liberation as a sequence of increasing subtlety. From another point of view, these are merely different modes, different expressions of the same face. Primordially liberated refers to the awakened state, but if you are talking about dualistic mind, it is not primordially freed. It needs to be liberated. The moment of dualistic mind needs to be dissolved, purified. The awakened state is not like this; it is already purified and fully perfected, so it does not have to be perfected.

When a reflection appears in a mirror, you do not have to imagine that it is there; it is vividly perceived. In the same way, you do not have to imagine basic wakefulness; it is naturally present. When a master performs the empowerment of enlightened mind, conferring the empowerment of nondual wakefulness to your dualistic mind, your thought activity is seen to be a "self-arising self-liberation." All thought activity occurs as the expression of awareness. By recognizing its source, it dissolves back into the state of awareness itself.

Thoughts occur as an expression of your essence, and not from anywhere else. They do not arise from the five elements, from the five sense organs, from flesh, blood, temperature, the heat or breath of your body — not at all. They are simply the expression of the primordially pure essence. Once you recognize your essence to be primordial purity, the thoughts that arise from yourself dissolve back into yourself, within the expanse of your nature. They do not go anywhere else. This is what is meant by self-arising self-liberation. If you do not know your essence, then what arises from yourself does not dissolve within yourself. Rather than being liberated, it goes astray into the six realms of samsara.

This is really the key point here. The thinking of dualistic mind arises or takes place as the expression of [unrecognized] awareness. Once you recognize this basic awareness, the display of thoughts loses all power and simply dissolves into the expanse of buddha nature. This is the basic reason to recognize mind essence.

Where does a thought come from? It occurs only as the display of your nature; it does not come from any other source. Look into this matter for a billion years, and you will never see a thought arise out of earth, water, fire or wind. Or out of a body — after all, even a corpse has flesh. There are cavities in the body, blood, heat, and so forth, but these components do not give rise to thoughts. Neither do thoughts arise from the objects perceived, whether they be visual forms, sounds, smells, tastes or textures. We have the five sense objects, and our body's five sense organs acting as go-betweens. A corpse has sense organs: it has eyes, but it does not see. It has ears, but it does not hear. It has a tongue, but it does not taste. It has a nose, but it does not smell. It has a body, but it does not feel. A corpse notices nothing. So, can't we conclude that the basis for every experience is our own minds? Isn't it only mind which knows?

That which knows is, in essence, empty. It is cognizant by nature, and its capacity is unconfined. Try to see this for yourself and understand that this is how your essence is. Thoughts arise from yourself and dissolve into yourself; they don't arise from yourself and dissolve somewhere else. Thoughts arise from yourself and, if you recognize their source, they dissolve into yourself as well. So, what is recognized, when we say "recognize'? It means seeing that the nature of mind is unconfined empty cognizance. This is the real condition, the natural state of the three kayas.

Realize this to be the real condition of things as they actually are, not just how they seem. The seeming way is created by our normal rigid and fixating thoughts. Recognize the real state, and this seeming way vanishes. These are the two aspects: the real and the seeming, the ultimate and the relative. The real is your essence; the seeming is your thoughts. Once you recognize the real state, the seeming way vanishes without a trace. It collapses, dissolves, completely vanishes. That's what this training is all about.

As I mentioned before, the moment of recognizing nondual awareness is called the identity of the three kayas. Our essence, nature and capacity are the dharmakaya, sambhogakaya and nirmanakaya. They are also the three vajras — the vajra body, speech and mind of all the buddhas — which we are supposed to achieve. This real and authentic state is, in itself, empty, which is dharmakaya. Its cognizant quality, isn't that sambhogakaya? Its unconfined unity, isn't that nirmanakaya? This indivisible identity of the three kayas is called the "essence body," *svabhavikakaya*. So, in this way, don't you have the three kayas right in the palm of your own hand? Why would you have to seek them out anywhere else? These three vajras are the basis for the body, speech and mind of all sentient beings as well. There are no sentient beings who are without body, speech and mind.

It is our thinking that causes us to continue in samsara. The moment of recognizing the identity of the three kayas is free from thought. This is what we should gain confidence in. At the beginning, the genuine recognition of the nature of mind is only a short moment, but it is indeed free from thought. When this state becomes unceasing, how can any of the three poisons exist? Is there any greater quality than that? This original wakefulness is often described in these words: "Free from thought, yet everything is vividly known." If there were no wakeful quality, it would be pointless to be free from thought; then it would be nothing but a vacant, dull state.

All the great qualities of buddhahood — the wisdom, compassion, and the capability to benefit others — all arise from this original wakefulness. Let's return to the word *sangye,* the Tibetan term for "buddha" which literally means "purified perfection." Dualistic consciousness tainted with the five poisons is purified, while the innate abundance of wisdom qualities is perfected. This is also called awakening or enlightenment.

This is, in short, the essence or very heart of the "three words that strike the vital point." If you want more details, you can read the whole *Tripitaka,* the commentaries of the masters, the 100,000 Nyingma tantras and so forth. A great master once said, "All the thousands of books and scriptures are taught for the sole purpose of realizing these Three Words." The Buddha's sole purpose for giving teachings is to enable us to recognize our empty, cognizant nature, to train in that and to attain stability.

The blacksmith may swing his hammer in all directions, but he must always land it directly on the anvil. In the same way, the Buddha gave all different kinds of teachings, but they all boil down to a single point. Although the blacksmith swings his hammer around in the air, he intends to strike a single point on the anvil. The hammer striking that spot on the anvil is like the "three words that strike the vital point."

What do we mean by vital point? If you want to kill someone, the physical body has its vital points; for instance, the heart. If you want to kill or cut the life-force of deluded thinking, there is no method other than recognizing buddha nature. How do you kill someone? Cutting off the arms and legs will not readily kill the person, will it? Stabbing him in the foot will not kill him either. But if you stab him directly in the heart, by the time you pull the knife out your victim is already dead. If you want to kill the delusion of samsara, your weapon is these Three Words.

There is another proverb from Kham about a mountain called Ngomo Langtang that is at the edge of a very vast plain. When people walk towards it, it always seems to be just in front of them, regardless of how far they travel. "Within one day's walk, Ngomo Langtang is visible. Within two day's walk, Ngomo Langtang is still visible." The distance is so vast it seems as though you are not getting any closer. In the same way, when I give a teaching, I speak about just this point and when I give another teaching, I again speak about just this. It is like the chirp of a small sparrow. A sparrow chirps in the same manner every day. My teaching is always the same. I chirp one day and on the following day I make the very same chirp.

SPACE

Two basic principles in the innermost Dzogchen teachings are space and awareness, in Tibetan *ying* and *rigpa*. Ying is defined as unconstructed space devoid of concepts, while rigpa means the "knowing" of that basic space.

In the context of the threefold sky practice, outer ying is defined as a clear sky free from the three defects of clouds, mist and haze. This external sky is an example for the actual inner ying and is used as a support for recognizing this state. The inner ying is the nature of mind, a state that is already empty. And the innermost ying, or basic space, is the recognition of buddha nature. The innermost ying is actually rigpa, nondual awareness itself.

We use the cloudless outer space as the example because it is without support — in it, there is nothing upon which the mind can fixate, or grasp at. It is unbased, unlike all the other elements. A clear pure sky is ideal for this practice: because it is vast and open it is without any support for thoughts. However, it is said that the ocean or a great lake can be used, if its surface is quiet and calm. A huge body of water can also serve as the object without support.

The reason the sky should be clear is that there should be no place or thing upon which to focus. It's a little different when the sky is cloudy, but it does not really make any difference because it is just an example. The space or sky in front of one, even if it's confined in a tiny room, has no support. Space is essentially open and free. Since both the sky and the lake are examples, their particular form doesn't really matter, as long as the meaning is recognized.

To reiterate, the outer space is the clear sky. The inner space is the primordial purity of empty mind essence. The innermost space is the knowing of this, which is the nondual awareness itself. When training with space, do not remain in thoughts: remain in awareness.

Ying likewise implies "not arising, not dwelling and not ceasing." Ultimately, all phenomena, whatever appearances we perceive, are beyond arising, dwelling and ceasing. The mind that perceives is also called *ying,* in the sense that mind is, by itself, empty. It is beyond arising, dwelling and ceasing. It does not come from anywhere; it doesn't remain anywhere; it doesn't go anywhere. This describes the inner ying.

Everything that is perceived as an object is ultimately "ying," basic space. Needless to say, most things don't appear this way to us. Therefore the other four elements, earth, water, fire and wind, are not used as an example, only the element of space itself, which is easily comprehended as being empty. Still, the other four elements are inherently empty. If we investigate where earth, water, fire and wind come from, we will not find a source. Look very closely: is there a place where earth comes from? Where water comes from? Where wind and fire initially come from? Right at this moment, is there an ultimate place where the four major elements are located? Try to find that. Is there a certain location that the four elements vanish into? Can we say, "They disappeared into such-and-such a place"? They are actually beyond arising, dwelling and ceasing. That describes the outer ying, the basic space of whatever is perceived. When we discover that all external objects composed of the four elements do not arise from anywhere, do not dwell anywhere and do not cease into some place — that everything is totally beyond arising, dwelling and ceasing — that is called "discovering the basic space of external phenomena."

Similarly, when looking into mind, the thinker, where does it come from? Where does it dwell? Where does it disappear to? In this way, we will discover the inner space that is totally beyond arising, dwelling and ceasing. So: if external space is beyond arising, dwelling and ceasing and inner space is beyond arising, dwelling and ceasing, how can we make any distinction between the two? Any separation is only a matter of two different names.

Everything we perceive is made out of visual forms, sounds, smells, tastes and textures. Look into these and investigate, "Where do these arise from? Where do they dwell? Where do they go to?" When we really examine this, we find there is no such thing as coming into being, dwelling anywhere, or disappearing. On a coarse level, the four major elements of earth, water, fire and wind, and on a more subtle perceptual level, all perceived objects of form, sound, smell, taste and texture are all discovered to be by nature beyond arising, dwelling and ceasing. When both the perceived objects and the perceiving subject are found to be beyond arising, dwelling and ceasing — utterly empty — everything is then just basic space. This is what is referred to as ying. In Sanskrit, the word is *dhatu.*

Ying and *yeshe,* basic space and wakefulness, are primordially indivisible, because our basic state is the unity of emptiness and cognizance. This is called the unity of space and wakefulness. The cognizant quality in this unity is called rigpa — awareness.

This basic state, the unity of being empty and cognizant, is at the very heart of all sentient beings. It is inherent within the thinking that takes place in all sentient beings at any moment. All beings possess this nature that is the unity of space and wakefulness, but, not knowing this, it doesn't help them. Instead of being suffused with awareness that knows itself, sentient beings become entangled in conceptualizing subject and object, thereby constantly and endlessly creating further states of samsara. All this occurs because they do not know their own nature.

This unity of space and wakefulness is sometimes called Samantabhadra, the Primordial Protector. Some people think that this basic space is totally vacant, and that consciousness is something separate from that. But this is not true. Basic space and wakefulness are primordially an indivisible unity. The basic space is like water and the wakefulness is like the wetness of water. Who can separate the wetness from water? If space were a flame, then wakefulness would be its heat. Who can separate heat from a flame? In the same way, basic space is always accompanied by basic wakefulness. Wakefulness is always accompanied by space. You cannot have one without the other; to think so would be a misunderstanding. To hammer it in, if space is sugar, then wakefulness is its sweetness. They are forever inseparable. This *dhatu,* or basic space, is the unity of being empty and cognizant. In the same way, rigpa is the unity of emptiness and cognizance.

The knowing of this nature that lies beyond complexity or constructs is called rigpa. Buddhas are empty cognizance suffused with awareness, the knowing quality, whereas the state of mind of sentient beings is empty cognizance suffused with ignorance, with unknowing. We cannot say there is any sentient being whose mind is not, at its core, the unity of emptiness and cognizance. But by not knowing this unity, their minds become a state of empty cognizance suffused with ignorance.

There are two ways to understand the view: inference and direct perception. Inference means intellectual understanding of the view. In terms of development stage and completion stage, the development stage is inference, while completion stage is direct perception. By resting freely, by utterly letting be, the empty and cognizant unity suffused with awareness is vividly present. Here "vividly" means directly, not governed by dualistic fixation.

To return to the threefold sky practice. First of all, the outer empty space is simply the openness right in front of you. The inner space of empty mind is simply the empty quality of your mind. The innermost space of empty rigpa, nondual awareness, is the moment traditionally spoken of as "four parts without three." This last is what is pointed out by the guru. To try to practice this without having received the pointing-out instruction and recognized rigpa is to mingle only two, not three types of space. There are only two spaces because, whether you recognize it or not, the space outside is always empty. The space of mind is always and forever empty. There is no question about that. Is outer space composed of anything? Is your mind composed of some concrete thing? That which is without concreteness is called "empty." To train in this without having recognized rigpa, is merely a mingling of two, not the threefold space. This is what happens whenever an ordinary person relaxes and looks into the sky.

But here, the practice is called "mingling the threefold space," not only the twofold space. Once you recognize rigpa, it is possible to mingle the outer, inner and innermost space. Otherwise, it becomes an intellectual exercise in thinking, "There's the empty sky outside. Now, here's the empty sky within. Now, I need the space of rigpa; then, I'll mingle all three together at once." It's not like this at all. To train in this fashion is called "mingling three concepts." There is one concept of a sky outside, a second concept of mind inside, and a third concept that empty rigpa must somehow appear. But actually, it is like this: you don't need to assume control of space outside. You don't need to take charge of the space within. Simply and totally disown all three — outer, inner, and the innermost space of rigpa. It is not like they need to be deliberately mingled; they are already mingled.

Your eyes need to connect with space; so do not look down at the ground but direct them upwards towards space. It's certain that the mind is inherently empty, so just leave this empty mind within rigpa. This is called "already having mingled the threefold space." In this state, it is possible to be free from fixation, but any deliberate attempt to mingle the three spaces is always fixation — thinking of space outside, thinking of space within, and then thinking, "I should mingle these two and then add rigpa." We should not call this "mingling the threefold space," but instead "mingling the threefold concepts." And if we equate the three concepts with the state of rigpa, it makes concepts seem more important than non-conceptual awareness, rigpa.

Why should we engage in this threefold sky practice? Space, by itself, is totally unconfined. There is no center and no edge in any direction whatsoever. Directing the gaze into the midst of empty space is an aid for allowing oneself to experience the similarly unconfined and all-pervasive state of rigpa.

Outer space transcends arising, dwelling and ceasing: this is the example for the awareness that is all-pervasive and empty, that like space, has no end. So mingle means and knowledge. Simply leave the state of mind that you have recognized suspended within unconfined external space. The means is space, the sky; the knowledge is the awareness which has been pointed out by one's master. When suspended like this, you don't need not try to mingle space and awareness — they are already mingled, premixed.

In the ultimate sense, space and awareness are a unity. Placing unfixated awareness in supportless space serves as an enhancement for the view. That is why it is said that one should practice outside. It's best to go to a high mountain-top so that when you look out you can see sky even below where you are sitting. A vast, wide-open vista is of great benefit for understanding the view. The great Drugpa Kagyü master Lorepa, spent 13 years living on an island in one of the four great lakes of Tibet. He said using the surface of water as a support free of focal point brought him great benefit.

To reiterate, perceptions or appearances are empty; the perceiver, the mind, is also empty. Consequently, ying and rigpa are a unity. At present, however, we have split ying and rigpa up into two, into "this here" and "that there," and we do not have this unity. Doesn't it seem to us that appearances and mind are two different things? Everything seems at present to be dualistic — perceived objects and the perceiving mind — and this perception endures as long as we have conceptual thinking. That is why there are so many references regarding the unity of space and awareness in Tibetan Buddhism.

We should understand ying in the sense of both outer and inner space. The four major elements are devoid of arising, dwelling and ceasing. The mind or consciousness is also devoid of arising, dwelling and ceasing. Since both are free from arising, dwelling and ceasing, they are a unity. How can we understand this? Think of the example of the space inside and outside a vase; then imagine what happens when the vase is shattered. There is a very important meaning contained in the prayer, "May we realize the unity of space and awareness!"

Everything with concrete substance is called "form," and all forms are the unity of appearance and emptiness: that is what is meant by vajra body. All sounds are resounding and yet empty: this is the vajra speech. When we recognize awareness, we realize that it is free from arising, dwelling and ceasing. That is the vajra mind. Whatever is devoid of arising, dwelling and ceasing is empty. This is exactly what is meant by the famous statement in the *Chöying Dzö,* that "everything seen, heard or thought is the adornment of space, and appears as the continuity of Body, Speech and Mind." In short, everything, without the exception of even a single dust mote, is of the nature of the three vajras.

Take my mala as an example. It can be thrown against the table and it seems as though it has physical form. Similarly, earth, water, fire and wind appear to possess physical form, but "form is emptiness," as the Buddha said. Even though it seems that forms exist, they do not possess true existence; they are empty of it. The basic fact is that they can all be destroyed. Everything will be destroyed in the end, the whole world and all its different elements. All these were formed at some point, they remain for some time and eventually they will disintegrate, to be followed by a period of complete voidness. These four periods of formation, remaining, disintegration and voidness are equal in length.

Even now, when considering whatever seems to us as being form, the proof that it is already an empty form is the fact that it will disintegrate. "Form is emptiness" means that whatever we perceive now, whatever seems to be solid form, is merely empty form, form empty of any inherent being. The next thing the Buddha said was, "Emptiness is also form," meaning although all things are empty, still they appear as form. This might not seem credible to us. It seems completely contradictory with what we perceive, and is not very easy to understand. But all things are already empty. In the ultimate sense, they do not come into being, they do not remain anywhere, and therefore they do not cease — that is to say, all things are beyond arising, dwelling and ceasing.

Another statement used is "Sense-objects are mere perception and therefore do not have concrete existence." That's a very important statement to remember. All sense-objects are "mere perceptions," and therefore do not exist. Whatever appears due to causes and conditions is ultimately nothing but a moment of mere perception. Perception never really arises or comes into being, it never remains, and therefore it never ceases to be.

Therefore, everything is *ying,* basic space beyond arising, dwelling and ceasing. All outer perceived objects are actually space that neither arises, remains nor ceases. At the same time, the perceiving mind is beyond arising, dwelling and ceasing as well. It is not some "thing" that comes into being, remains or ceases. So, it is not only the mind that is empty while the objects are real and concrete. If that were true, there could not be any mingling of space and awareness. Both the outside and the inside, both perceived objects and the perceiving subject, are already beyond arising, dwelling and ceasing. Therefore, it *is* possible to train in mingling space and awareness.

SAMAYA

A S YOU KNOW, THERE ARE DIFFERENT VEHICLES for shravakas, bodhi-sattvas, and followers of Secret Mantra. Each has their respective precepts, trainings and samayas. When condensed to the essence, the very heart of all these samayas is contained in the four samayas of the Dzogchen view — nonexistence, all-pervasiveness, oneness and spontaneous perfection — and the three root samayas of Body, Speech and Mind.

As Vajrayana practitioners, we abide by all these three sets of principles. For instance, we take refuge at the very beginning of any empowerment, and have therefore received the refuge precepts of the shravakas. After that, we form the bodhichitta resolve and so also receive the bodhisattva precepts. As for Secret Mantra, the moment we drink the "samaya water," the drops of water from the conch given out before the actual empowerment, the water is transformed into Vajrasattva, who rests in the center of our hearts. When we keep the samayas we are never separate from Vajrasattva.

A good way to describe Vajrayana samayas is to use the example of a snake in the hollow of a bamboo shaft. The snake can neither go right nor left; it must either go up or down. Going up describes what is called the "upward directness" which indicates we are ready to enter a buddhafield. On the other hand, there is the "downward directness" which applies to those who break the samaya vows. I hate to mention this, but such a person can only go downward into the three lower realms. This is precisely what is meant by the tremendous benefit or the correspondingly huge risks involved in the Vajrayana samayas.

To be Vajrayana practitioners we must have received the four empowerments, which in themselves are the very heart of the path of Secret Mantra. We have entered the Vajrayana path simply by receiving these four empowerments. In other words, the snake has already crept into the bamboo shaft. If you keep the samayas you gain supreme accomplishment. If not, then that which remained as Buddha Vajrasattva in the center of your heart as long as you observed the purity of samaya transforms itself into a "fierce yaksha," a [self-destructive] force that shortens your life-span and "consumes the vital essences of your heart-blood." This is the way to inescapably propel yourself into the "downward directness" at the end of your life.

The practice of Secret Mantra is the short-cut, the swiftest path to reaching the inconceivable common and supreme accomplishments. As you move up through the different vehicles, the "narrow defile" of this path of samaya grows increasingly confined; there is less and less room to move, so be on guard.. In the case of a shravaka or bodhisattva, it is more simple to progress: keep virtuous and disciplined in thought, word and deed — stay on guard against unwholesome behavior, adopt what is good. The samayas of Vajrayana, on the other hand, is to never let your body depart from being the deity, your voice from being mantra and your mind from the state of samadhi. If you are able to do so, that is keeping the ultimate samayas with the Body, Speech and Mind of the victorious ones. You can then truly be said to possess the sacred precepts of Vajrayana. Without doing so, understand that the samayas of Secret Mantra hold extreme risk.

There are as well the samayas with the vajra master: not to disparage his bodily presence, break his command or upset his feelings. Let me again summarize about the different samayas. Concerning your vajra master, do not disrespect his bodily presence, his word, or his feelings. Moreover do not separate your body from being the deity, your voice from mantra and your mind from samadhi.

As for "vajra siblings," there are three kinds: distant, close and very close. The very close brothers and sisters are the ones together with whom you received instructions on mind essence at the feet of the same master. Close vajra siblings are the people with whom you have taken the same empowerments and oral instructions. The distant siblings are for instance the people who were also present in a huge Dharma gathering or empowerment assembly, sometimes numbering into the thousands. We must keep our samaya with all these brothers and sisters, staying clear of perceiving them as imperfect, harboring resentment, ridiculing or belittling one another, criticizing behind each other's back, or the like. If you can keep completely clean and tidy, without all those defects, you can be said to have pure samaya.

Ultimately, to be totally free from any defects in your vows and samayas, you need to remain in the continuity of the four samayas of the Dzogchen view — nonexistence, all-pervasiveness, oneness and spontaneous perfection. If you are able to fulfill these you totally transcend any possible violation or breach of samaya. Nonexistence and all-pervasiveness are the two samayas of Trekchö, while oneness and spontaneous perfection are the samayas of Tögal. To accomplish this you need to be able to dissolve dualistic mind in nondual awareness, rigpa.

This nondual awareness is the very identity of the three kayas of the awakened state of buddhahood. Within it all three — dharmakaya, sambhogakaya and nirmanakaya — are complete. The three vajras of all buddhas — the unchanging vajra body, the unceasing vajra speech and the unmistaken vajra mind — are complete within it as well. When you remain in the fourfold samaya of nonexistence, all-pervasiveness, oneness and spontaneous perfection, not a single infraction or transgression of samaya is possible, not even as much as a hair-tip. Until this point, however, there is no avoiding incurring breaches of samaya, be they subtle or coarse.

In the general classifications of samaya you find the four stages called infraction, transgression, violation, and breach [literally: contradicting, damaging, breaking, and passing]. These categories depend in part on the length of time which has passed since the samaya was damaged. After three years of still not having apologized, there is no longer any chance to mend the samaya. At this point it is overstepped and becomes irreparable.

The precepts and trainings of the Sutra system, including both Hinayana and Mahayana, are difficult to repair once they are broken, like an earthen pot dropped on the ground. But according to the vajra vehicle of Secret Mantra, if you sincerely try to mend a break in samaya, it is like repairing the dent in a golden vase. A scratch or dent in a vase of silver or gold can be immediately repaired, but can you put together a clay pot once it breaks? There is immense danger in being careless about one's samayas. However, when sincerely and genuinely mending them with apology and resolution, then the damage is similar to a dent in a golden vessel; it can easily be repaired.

Most important is the samaya with the guru; next is that with the vajra brothers and sisters. Everyone, both master and disciples, must keep the samayas. When this is done correctly and purely, the outcome is extremely profound. There is a saying among the masters of the past, "Samaya violation is my worst enemy; the guru is my best friend." The real enemy is the breaking of samaya; it can damage the master's health and life. The breach of samaya among close or distant vajra brothers and sisters also creates negative karma and misfortune.

Broken samaya really does have an impact for both master and disciples. It creates unhappiness and turmoil that prevents one from remaining in the state of samadhi. In other words, impaired samaya hinders the training in samadhi and creates obstacles for learning, reflection and meditation. Broken samaya is definitely detrimental to health, happiness and all other positive qualities.

"Samaya violation is my worst enemy; the guru is my best friend." This statement by the great Kagyü masters means that the only enemy they could not contend with is someone tainted by the defilement from broken samayas, and that the most eminent companion is their qualified master. Isn't this the difference samaya makes?

In short, the best way to keep the samayas intact is through the proper view, meditation and conduct. If that is not completely possible, patience is a strong basis for keeping samayas. It is said, "Don't retaliate with anger when attacked with rage. Don't retaliate with abuse when reviled. Don't retaliate with criticism when blamed in public. Don't retaliate with blows when threatened with physical violence." Be patient even if someone actually hits you. If you can be forbearing in this way, you will triumph over the enemy of broken samayas. Otherwise, if each attack has to be met with revenge, if each hurtful word must be matched with another spiteful word, the cycle never ends. One might think, "I am right!" and say something in return, but the other person will think, "You are wrong!" and counter with more abuse, and so on.

There is an Eastern Tibetan saying, "Words are the wellspring of all strife." This is the main reason for staying in silent retreat. The voice is the instigator of quarrels. No one can know what you think inside, only buddhas and bodhisattvas. But the tongue, being as nasty as it is, [Rinpoche laughs] does not want to stay silent, and so begin all kinds of quarrels.

The main point is, therefore, to be your own teacher. When someone attacks you, do not fight back in any way whatsoever. Stay as quiet as a stone; this will allow you to triumph over squabbles. What does it truly matter what other people say? The way of worldly people is give tit for tat, to respond in kind; someone attacks you, so you fight back. That is how disputes begin. The best way, really, is to keep your mouth shut as tightly as a squeezed ball of tsampa.

The vajra vehicle of Secret Mantra has the potential for great reward, but also for great danger. The great reward is that authentic practice of the oral instructions enables us to reach complete enlightenment at what is called the unified level of a vajra-holder, within this same body and lifetime. The great danger lies in the fact that nothing is more risky than the samayas. Isn't this true? Once "the snake is in the shaft," there are only two openings to exit from, the top or the bottom: there is no third alternative. Once you take the empowerments, you are caught in the bamboo-shaft of the samayas. And isn't it true that in order to be a Vajrayana practitioner there is no way around receiving empowerment?

Now, there are some people who, while calling themselves Vajrayana practitioners, mistakenly believe they do not have to observe any of the precepts of individual liberation, the bodhisattva trainings or the vidyadhara samayas of Secret Mantra. How can that be correct? Is there any empowerment ceremony that excludes taking refuge? In the moment of committing yourself to the Three Jewels — whether or not they are described in detail — you implicitly receive the Hinayana precepts. Don't you repeat three times the lines of the bodhisattva vow as well? Contained within the meaning of that is the entire body of bodhisattva trainings, in principle if not in letter.

The vase empowerment of Secret Mantra authorizes you to practice the development stage. Through the secret empowerment and the wisdom-knowledge empowerment you are entitled to train in the two aspects of completion stage with characteristics. Lastly, through the precious word empowerment, you are authorized to practice the entire path of Trekchö and Tögal, of primordial purity and spontaneous presence. In fact, once you receive these four empowerments, you have in reality received authorization for the entire path. Having received in principle the entire body of teachings of the three vehicles, how can one claim, "I don't have to keep any precepts!"? To abide by the precepts, one definitely has to observe the samayas.

On another note, for a layperson it will suffice as "samaya" if he or she can just keep to the ten virtuous actions. But perhaps you want to rise above the state of an ordinary person and become a noble being. All the tools, all the precepts and samayas for this are included within the empowerment ritual of Vajrayana. You need to take refuge, generate bodhichitta, and receive the four empowerments.

Having received empowerment, you want to maintain the connection by keeping these precepts, though you may not be an amazingly great practitioner. But if you manage to keep the samayas intact, you will be able to have the six recollections when you roam through the bardo state after death. These include remembering the guru, the oral instructions, the yidam deity, and so forth. Conversely, someone who damaged and then broke off his or her samaya commitments will have the experience of being shrouded in dense fog, and will be totally bewildered. He or she will not know what to do, what to trust or where to go in the bardo. Such an individual will definitely be unable to remember what counts, in terms of the six recollections.

You may not have done extensive meditation on the yidam deity or performed many mantra recitations. Even so, if you have maintained sincere trust and have not spoiled your samayas, you can still be benefited by the fourfold liberation of Secret Mantra in the bardo, and proceed to a higher path. These four are liberation through seeing, hearing, remembering or touching. They are not possible for someone who throws the sacred commitments of samaya to the winds and pretentiously exclaims, "I am a meditator, I have accomplishment." The four liberations unquestionably depend on the purity of samaya. Thus, it is much better to be a simple practitioner who has not violated his or her samaya, even though he may not have a particularly high view or deep meditation. Through his pure samaya commitment he is able to journey along the straight path towards liberation from samsara and complete enlightenment.

When we look around us, the consequences of people's actions and their keeping or breaking of samaya is not something that is immediately visible. It is quite possible for us to think, "My vows are whole and intact; I have not broken anything; I am pure and clean; I am a righteous person!" If we keep up such a pretense, we are totally incapable of seeing our faults. But unfortunately, we damage and violate the samayas repeatedly. We need to acknowledge our faults to be able to remedy them; this is important.

Come to your senses and think well about this. Understand that damaged samayas will hurt you in future lives. To deal with this issue, you have to acknowledge your own shortcomings, don't you? Without admitting any personal fault, it is as Jamgön Kongtrül says in his *Calling the Guru From Afar:* "Though my faults are as huge as a mountain, I hide them within. Though others" faults are as tiny as mustard seeds, I proclaim them far and wide. Even though I do not possess any good qualities, I still pretend to be virtuous." Most people fall prey to this shortcoming.

Gampopa also said, "When the Dharma is not practiced correctly, it becomes a cause for returning to the lower realms." This is very true. Practicing the Dharma correctly means keeping pure samayas, and developing devotion to those above, compassion for those below and being diligent at all times. The most eminent training is to recognize the wish-fulfilling jewel of your own mind. When you do all these things, then you will be able to cross safely through the bardo. There, through the kindness of the fourfold liberation you will be successful in traversing the bardo.

Otherwise, once you arrive in the bardo, you will find no one to be pretentious with, lie to or deceive. It is like the metaphor of the "revealing mirror" that clearly shows all your deeds. Failure or success in the bardo depends ultimately on the integrity of one's samaya. Those who have kept pure samaya will, through the above-mentioned fourfold liberation, definitely escape further roaming about in the three lower realms.

You may have an amazingly high level of view and realization; you may have attained a certain level of accomplishment and possess various types of totally unimpeded superknowledge. But the moment you violate your samayas, I'm sorry to say, you fall straight back down again. There is no way around that: the road upward is blocked.

Always scrutinize your own shortcomings. Ignore the faults of other people. Keep this attitude: "Whether they are pure or whether they are defiled, it is none of my business!" Be your own teacher; keep a strict check on yourself. That is sufficient! There is then no chance for a single error to sneak in.

On the other hand, maybe you want to go to the place which in the Sutra tradition is known as the Hell of Incessant Torment, and in Secret Mantra is called Vajra Hell. The only way is arrive there is to break your samayas. Ordinary evil deeds, even very negative ones, will not suffice. You cannot go there unless you violate the samayas. This is the uncompromising fact of the samayas. So if you want to take a sight-seeing tour to Vajra Hell, first you must diligently break your samayas, because ordinary misdeeds and obscuration will not suffice to get you there! [Rinpoche laughs] Then you'll get to see the Vajra Hell, with the other 18 hell realms thrown in for free. If you want to visit the dharmadhatu buddhafield of

Akanishtha, you have to keep your samayas pure. This is the serious truth involving the keeping and breaking of samaya.

Having entered the path of Vajrayana's four empowerments, train in bringing self-existing wakefulness into the realm of your experience. Moreover, triumph over being tainted by even the most subtle breach of samaya. If you can accomplish this, you will journey through the "upward directness." That means you will attain the state of complete enlightenment within your present body. Conversely, you may have received Vajrayana teachings but have let the time fly by while totally ignoring the sacredness of samaya. In this case, you will succeed in visiting the deepest pit of Vajra Hell. That is what is meant by no third alternative.

It is said that the buddhas are both skillful and compassionate in teaching the vajra vehicle of Secret Mantra. This implies there is the possibility of purification through apology and resolution. By apologizing from the bottom of your heart and resolving never to commit the transgression again, any misdeed, obscuration, violation or breach can be purified. This must take place before three years have passed; otherwise it is very hard. This is the only and primary quality of evil deeds: that they can be purified through apology and resolution.

That evil deeds can be purified through apology is one of the special qualities of Vajrayana. Take the instance of someone who has committed one of the "five acts with immediate result." Even these can be purified. In order to purify them, it is necessary for that person to arrange the mandala of the peaceful and wrathful buddhas; to invite a master with disciples in a corresponding number; and to offer them respect and make lavish offerings. Then, in their midst he must proclaim with a loud voice, "I have done such-and-such evil! I have committed the five acts with immediate result: killed my father and mother, killed an arhat, and the rest! There is no one worse then me! Please help me purify my misdeeds!" After exclaiming this, the person must strip off his clothes in the presence of the gathering and the mandala of the peaceful and wrathful deities, and make full prostrations while reciting the Hundred Syllable Mantra one hundred and eight times. Then the karma of even these five acts will be purified. This is what is meant by Vajrayana being incredibly skillful and compassionate.

All of us have already entered the gateway to Vajrayana by simply receiving one empowerment. Whether that empowerment was famous or not does not really matter; you receive the precepts and samayas by participating in any ceremony in which the four empowerments are given.

Violating the "pledged discipline," the oath to keep the Vajrayana precepts, is much worse than the "unformulated evil." Unformulated evil is what we might unwittingly commit if we are an ordinary person who has not taken any vows or commitments. There is nothing worse than failing to observe the pledge one has taken, since it is samaya violation that truly cuts the life-force of liberation.

The samayas include the connection with distant vajra brothers and sisters, like those who participate in the empowerment ceremony a grand master gives to a crowd of thousands. It also includes the connection with close siblings — those who live in the same monastery under the guidance of the same teacher. Finally there are the extremely close siblings, the ones with whom we received the teachings on mind essence. That is the most uncompromising; there is no one more intimate than these extremely close vajra brothers and sisters. We should regard them as being as precious as the heart in our chest or the eyes in our head.

The misdeeds and obscurations created through countless past lives must be purified through apology, otherwise there is no way in the world that they will disappear by themselves. These negative patterns lie dormant as habitual tendencies that sooner or later will manifest in our dualistic frame of mind. We must purify them with apology, which is always possible, as I mentioned when defining the only virtue of evil deeds. This is the purpose of the Hundred Syllable Mantra among the preliminary practices. In this, we apologize not only for the negative actions we have committed within this life and in this body; but for all the negative actions we have committed since beginningless time until now.

Unless we dispense with the dualistic frame of mind, these traces of misdeeds and obscurations remain as habitual tendencies that will reoccur within this dualistic attitude. They do not disappear otherwise: this is why you hear so often about the need for purification. You can definitely purify them all by means of the four powers in the Vajrasattva practice. Your negative karma may be as huge as Mount Sumeru but it can still be purified by apology. Imagine a mountain of dry grass the size of a mountain; doesn't it all burn down when set on fire?

It is also said, "Realization occurs automatically when misdeeds are purified." When your intrinsic buddha nature is free from any veil, it is naturally stable in itself. But normally it is obscured by unwholesome tendencies. Don't the clouds covering the sky make it impossible to clearly see the stars and planets?

It's impossible to train in and grow accustomed to the original wakefulness as long as we are unaware of it and fail to recognize it, or as long as we are caught up in doubt even if we have recognized it. On the other hand, once you completely arrive in nondistraction, the king of all samayas, you transcend the dividing line between keeping and breaking samaya. At that level there is no samaya whatsoever to observe. Until that happens, however, there is no way around observing the samayas, since we are still controlled by dualistic mind.

The dualistic frame of mind is what we need to be free from, and nondual awareness is the outcome of this freedom. As I have mentioned earlier, these two aspects coexist at present, but as we progressively purify our karmic misdeeds and obscurations, realization occurs spontaneously. Realization in this sense means that the stream of conceptual thinking becomes self-arising self-liberation, until finally your state of mind is like a cloudless, clear sky. At this point, since there is no more distraction, conceptual thinking is naturally liberated. This is the point when one transcends the dividing line between keeping and breaking samaya. This is also the point of realizing the four samayas of the Dzogchen view: nonexistence, all-pervasiveness, oneness and spontaneous perfection. You do not have to try to understand these individually, as they are inherently inseparable. But, up until this realization, isn't claiming "I don't break any samayas!" only pretentious self-deception?

APPLICATION

Buddhist practice involves three steps known as intellectual understanding, experience and realization. Intellectual understanding occurs when, for instance, we hear that emptiness, meaning empty cognizance, is our nature. The mental idea we get of this is called "understanding." In the case of experience, we are told how to recognize emptiness so that we can see exactly how this empty cognizance is. We have a taste of it, maybe no more than a glimpse, but, nevertheless, an experience of what is called "recognizing mind essence." That is what the word "experience" means in this context. When this glimpse is followed by training in repeatedly recognizing the nature of mind and avoiding being carried away by thoughts, we gradually grow more and more used to this experience. In this case, by recognizing the empty nature we are disengaging from its expression, the stream of deluded thinking. Each time the expression dissolves back into the state of awareness, progress is made, and realization finally occurs. Ultimate realization is when delusion has totally collapsed and there is no re-occurrence of discursive thought whatsoever.

Thoughts are like clouds and can vanish just as clouds naturally disperse into space. The expression, meaning thoughts, are like clouds, while rigpa is like sunlit space. I use the metaphor of sunlit space to illustrate that space and awareness are indivisible. You do not accomplish or create the sunlit sky. We cannot push the clouds away, but we can allow the clouds of thought to gradually dissolve until finally all the clouds have vanished. When it becomes easier to recognize, and when recognition is self-sustained, that can be called "realization." Ultimate realization occurs when there is no trace of the cloud layers whatsoever.

It is not as if we need to decide, "I hate these thoughts. I only want the awakened state! I have to be enlightened!" This kind of grasping and pushing will never give way to enlightenment. By simply allowing the expression of thought activity to naturally subside, again and again, the moments of genuine rigpa automatically and naturally begin to last longer. When there are no thoughts whatsoever, then you are a buddha. At that point the thought-free state is effortless, as well as the ability to benefit all beings. But until that time it does not help to think that you are a buddha. We need to become used to this natural dissolving of thought through training, like learning something by heart. Having become accustomed to it; the thoughtfree state becomes automatic.

Listening to this explanation is merely getting the idea. We intellectually comprehend that emptiness is empty yet cognizant and that these two aspects are indivisible. It is like going to a buffet where we don't actually taste anything, but only receive a guided tour or explanation of the different dishes: "This is Indian food, that is Chinese food. Over there is French cuisine." Without eating anything your knowledge of the food is only intellectual understanding. Once you finally put the food in your mouth, that is experience. When your stomach is full, that is realization. Realization is the total and permanent collapse of confusion.

Empty cognizance is our nature. We cannot separate one aspect of it from the other. Empty means "not made out of anything whatsoever'; our nature has always been this way. Yet, while being empty, it has the capacity to cognize, to experience, to perceive. It's not so difficult to comprehend this; to get the theory that this empty cognizance is buddha nature, self-existing wakefulness. But to leave it at that is the same as looking at the buffet and not eating anything. Being told about buddha nature but never really making it our personal experience will not help anything. It's like staying hungry. Once we put the food in our mouth, we discover what the food tastes like. This illustrates the dividing line between idea and experience.

In the same way, if we have correct understanding, the moment we apply what our master teaches, we recognize our nature. That there is no entity whatsoever to be seen is called "emptiness." The ability to know that mind essence is empty is called "cognizance." If it were only blank, bare space, what or who would know that it is "blank" or "empty" or "nothing"? There would be no knowing. These two aspects, empty and cognizant, are indivisible. This becomes obvious to us the very moment that we look; it is no longer hidden. Then it is not just an intellectual idea of how emptiness is; it becomes a part of our experience. At that moment, meditation training can truly begin.

We call this training "meditation," but it is not an act of meditating in the common sense of the word. There is no emptying the mind essence by trying to maintain an artificially imposed vacant state. Why? Because mind essence is already empty. Similarly, we do not need to make this empty essence cognizant; it is already cognizant. All you have to do is leave it as it is. In fact, there is nothing whatsoever to do, so we cannot even call this an act of meditating. There is an initial recognition, and from then on we do not have to be clever about it or try to improve it in any way whatsoever. Just let it be as it naturally is — that is what is called meditation, or more accurately "nonmeditation." What is crucial is not to be distracted for even a single instant. Once recognition has taken place, undistracted nonmeditation is the key point of practice.

"Distracted" means that once the attention wavers and loses itself, thoughts and emotions can take place: "I want to do such and such. I'm hungry. I want to go to that place. I wonder what I should say to this person; this is what I will say." Distraction is the return of all these kinds of thoughts, in which the continuity of nondual awareness is lost. The training is simply to recognize again. Once recognition takes place, there is nothing more to do; simply allow mind essence to be. That is how the cloud-covers gradually dissolve.

The ultimate state is totally free from any obscuration, like the short moment of recognition. However, in the latter there is still the tendency for the obscurations to return. The state of realization, complete enlightenment, means that no cloud-cover can ever return; its causes are utterly and permanently eliminated. When the clouds vanish, what else can cover the sun? That is the final or ultimate realization — when there is only brilliant, pure sunshine throughout space without any cloud-cover whatsoever. In other words, everything that needed to be removed has been removed and everything that needed to be actualized is already present. The empty sky and the brilliant sunshine are not of our making. They have always been there and are fully actualized when the cloud-cover is eliminated. Whatever had to be abandoned has, at this time, been abandoned. Whatever had to be realized, has been realized. So, what is left?

Ultimate realization, which is the third point, is achieved through repeating the short moment of recognition many times. When the recognition lasts continuously throughout the day we have reached the level of a bodhisattva. When it lasts uninterruptedly, day and night, we have attained buddhahood.

Here is another way to illustrate the differences between intellectual understanding, experience and realization. Imagine that you run around town saying, "All things are the unity of empty cognizance." Let's say you shout that loud and clear in the marketplace. Some people will think, "This person is crazy. How can all things be the unity of empty cognizance? That's complete nonsense! He's crazy!" But another person will think, "No, this is not nonsense. He's talking about how the mind is. There are no things separate from the perceiver, the mind itself. Mind is the unity of empty cognizance. Therefore, all things are the unity of empty cognizance. He is right!" This is the difference between having and not having the correct understanding.

"All things" in Sanskrit is *sarva dharma*. *Sarva* means all, myriad, manifold and *dharma* means appearances, phenomena, the perceived — all the contents of our experience, such as sights, sounds, smells, tastes, textures and so forth. Now, an ordinary person cannot possibly understand how all these things that are supposed to be "out there" can be empty cognizance. It does not make any sense. So he will naturally wonder what that madman in the marketplace was babbling about; this is a normal response. But a person who has some degree of understanding will say, "Things don't know themselves. There is nothing other than the mind that knows things. Things exist because of being perceived by a perceiving mind. This mind is empty and cognizant, therefore, all things are the unity of empty cognizance." Such comprehension is correct, yet it is still only intellectual understanding.

The second step, experience, is something more personal and not solely an idea. You have not merely heard that mind essence is empty and cognizant; rather, you recognize this empty essence in actuality when it's pointed out by the master and again whenever you remember. This sense of being awake and empty — that is experience.

At the moment of experience, what is recognized is not something new. Empty cognizance has always been present. It is often called "self-existing wakefulness," *rangjung yeshe*. It is not created by the mere recognition of it, or through the pointing-out instruction. It is your nature itself, your natural face. What a master does is simply tell you how to look. He merely points it out; *we* recognize and experience it. But some people refuse to understand this. They think, "First I must get rid of my nasty old dualistic mind. I must discard it so that the amazing buddha mind can come down from above, like a beautiful god dissolving into me. Then, I'm sure, something spectacular will happen. That's what recognizing buddha nature is, not just seeing nothing." In this way, some people simply refuse to recognize their nature. They think, "How can this ordinary state of mind be anything special? There must be something wonderful that will happen at some time — maybe not now, but in the future." If one lies waiting for some fabulous vision to occur, one is simply molding the circumstances for some kind of demonic force to enter oneself. In terms of buddha-nature nothing very special is going to happen, because the real, true state is already present. It is not something new.

Please understand that there are three steps: recognizing, training and attaining stability. The first of these steps, recognizing, is like acquiring the seed of a flower. Once it is in your hands and you acknowledge it to be a flower, it can be planted and cultivated. When fully grown, flowers will bloom; but the seed needs the right conditions. However, we must first acknowledge that it is indeed a flower seed. In the same way, the naked awareness that has been pointed out by your master should be acknowledged as your nature. This recognition must be nurtured by the right conditions. To cultivate a seed, it must have warmth and moisture and so on; then it will certainly grow. In the same way, after recognizing we must train in the natural state: the short moment of recognition needs to be repeated many times. As the support for this training, have devotion to enlightened beings and compassion for unenlightened beings. Devotion and compassion are a universal panacea, the single sufficient technique. A famous quote says, "In the moment of love, the nature of emptiness dawns nakedly." Both compassion and devotion are included in the "love" mentioned here.

Training is simply short moments of recognition repeated many times and supported by devotion and compassion. In addition, there are practices called the development and completion stages. All these practices facilitate nondistraction. When you give water, warmth and protection to a sprouted seed, it will continue to grow. Repeatedly training in nondistraction is how to progress in the practice of mind nature.

Finally comes the stage of stability. When this moment of nondistraction lasts unceasingly, day and night, what will that be like? When the three poisons are obliterated and the qualities of wakefulness become fully manifest, will we be ordinary human beings or divine? A single candle-flame can set the whole of a mountainside ablaze. Imagine what it would be like when our present experience of the wide awake moment free from thought becomes unceasing. Is there anything more divine than possessing all the wisdom qualities and being utterly free from the three poisons?

We can deduce from this that training is needed. We must grow up, just like a new-born baby. The way for us to do this is through training. The infant born today and the adult 25 years later is essentially the same person, isn't he? He is not someone else. Right now, our nature is the buddha nature. When fully enlightened, it will also be the buddha nature. Our nature is unfabricated naturalness. It is this way by itself: like space, it does not need to be manufactured. Do we need to imagine or create the space in our room? It's the same with buddha nature. But we do need to allow the experience of buddha nature to continue through unfabricated naturalness.

Another example for our nature, which is unfabricated naturalness, is the sun shining. In ordinary beings, this sunshine turns into conceptual thinking that obscures the sun. Beings are carried away by their thoughts. If we simply let it be as it naturally is, without trying to modify, there is no way to err, no way to stray from the view. It's when we try to manufacture or do something that it becomes artificial. Check this out for yourself. Is the moment that you call your "nature" something that you need to make and then maintain in a busy, contrived way? Or is it sufficient to leave it as it naturally is? This is something you should examine for yourself.

If during your practice you start to think, "Well, this state is not exactly right, it needs to be a little different," or "I guess this is it." "Maybe this is not it!" or "Now I've got it!" "I just had it! Now it slipped away," this is not what I mean by unfabricated naturalness.

One sign of having trained in rigpa, the awakened state, is simply that conceptual thinking, which is the opposite of rigpa, grows less and less. The gap between thoughts grows longer and occurs more and more frequently. The state of unfabricated awareness, what the tantras call the "continuous instant of nonfabrication," becomes more and more prolonged. This continuity of rigpa is not something we have to deliberately maintain. It should occur spontaneously through having grown more familiar with it. Once we become accustomed to the genuine state of unfabricated rigpa, it will automatically start to last longer and longer.

What is meant by stability, then? First, to gain stability, we need to have recognized genuine rigpa. We should have clearly ascertained the true state. Through training, we should have gained some degree of stability in this so that we are no longer carried away by circumstances. These conditions can be either positive or negative. Negative circumstances like difficulties, mishaps or illness, are much easier to recognize and not be overcome by. Thus, it is easier to practice during times of difficulty than it is when being successful. The worst obstacle for a practitioner is when crowds of followers begin to gather and say, "You are so wonderful; you're such a great practitioner.

You are very special. Please give us teachings. Please guide us." Starting to have a great following causes the most difficult kind of obstacle because, unless one is the foremost type of practitioner, one will think, "Hey, maybe I am special. Maybe there is something to what they say." Only the foremost type of practitioner will not be carried away by such "positive" conditions. When we reach the point of being carried away by neither positive or negative circumstances, we have gained some stability.

There are signs of accomplishment, such as having good health and long life or becoming famous and influential, but these belong to the superficial type of accomplishment. The true, unmistaken signs of accomplishment as established by the masters of the lineage, are to possess compassion, devotion and an acute sense of impermanence. Combined with this, thoughts grow less and less and the genuine awakened state lasts for increasingly longer periods.

All doubts or uncertainties concerning the view of rigpa should be cleared up. When we are free of doubts, there is nothing to clear up. Doubt is the obstacle that obstructs the view. If there is no obstacle, there is also nothing to clear away. Jigmey Lingpa said, "When you do not lose the innate stability of awareness even if you [are questioned by] a hundred great masters or a thousand scholars, then no doubt remains to clear up."

At some point along the path to enlightenment, daytime delusion vanishes. Eventually, even at night-time one does not fall back into the pattern of deluded thinking. All phenomena and conceptual states dissolve back into the primordially pure state of dharmata. This is the dharmakaya itself, from which the two rupakayas, sambhogakaya and nirmanakaya, spontaneously manifest for the welfare of sentient beings, infinitely and endlessly. But, until that happens, there is still training to be undergone.

We need to gradually dispense with conceptual thinking. It would be best, of course, if we could simply cut right through at this moment and never again become involved with thoughts. But are we able to throw them away? In the moment of unfabricated awareness thoughts do not have the power to remain, because that instant is totally free from the duality of perceiver and perceived. In the flame of nondual awareness, the hair of conceptual thinking cannot remain: just as a single hair cannot remain in a flame, a thought cannot possibly remain in the recognition of the awakened state. What we call *sem*, dualistic mind, is always involved in upholding the concepts of perceiver and perceived. Rigpa, however, is by nature devoid of duality. The whole basis for the continuance of conceptual thinking is duality. If the concepts of perceiver and perceived are not kept up, duality crumbles, and there is no way conceptual thinking can continue.

Our conceptual thinking is like a sneak-thief who can only rob by stealth. Try this; in broad daylight in a gathering of many people invite the thief in to steal whatever he wants. The thief will be unable to pilfer anything.

The bottom line is to try, as much as possible, to retain the innate stability of nondual awareness, of that continuous instant of nonfabrication. Do not create or construct anything whatsoever; simply allow the moment of rigpa to reoccur repeatedly. If you train in this with utmost diligence, you can fully achieve the state of enlightenment after no more than a few years. Even if you are not that caliber of practitioner and practice moderately, you will at the very least be able to die without regret.

It's not hard to gain some intellectual understanding of the Dharma; as they say, talk is cheap. Anyone can talk about it. One can easily say, "The awakened state is amazing. It is endowed with all perfect qualities, totally free from any faults. In fact, nothing can ever harm the state of rigpa. It is totally untainted." Or it is very easy to say, "Everything is illusion. The whole world is merely an illusion. Nothing has any independent or true existence. It's all magical trickery." We can deliver these words from our mouths, but this is not enough to destroy the state of confusion, to make our delusion fall apart. To do this, we need the genuine experience.

Experience here, means to recognize the essence that is like space. In the moment of rigpa, any deluded state is seen as baseless, illusory and rootless. The false nature of thought becomes totally obvious, in a very immediate and personal way that is not just an idea that we have heard. At that moment we directly touch the truth of those statements. By attaining stability in this direct experience, the great masters of the Kagyü lineage could make statements like, "The rock here is totally transparent. Everything is the magical trickery of illusion." Due to their level of realization, these masters could pass through solid rock, drill themselves into the ground, walk on water, fly through the air and so forth. This was not because they had developed some special powers through their practice or because they were very strong or stubborn but simply because everything is unreal from the very outset. Because of realizing the insubstantial nature of things, as it is, practitioners have been able to manifest such signs of accomplishment. Otherwise, we can study the teachings and say pithy things like, "There is nothing to worry about in the bardo. Everything that then occurs is an illusion; there is nothing real about it." But when we eventually arrive in the bardo states, we will be completely embroiled in the raging river of our fear.

Let me reiterate the three steps, intellectual understanding, experience and realization. Intellectual understanding is, for instance, to have heard about the awakened state. Theory, is, of course, important, and we should definitely know the intent of the teachings. However, we should not leave it with that. We need to incorporate all three: theory, experience and realization.

Then there is recognizing, training and attaining stability. Of these three, "recognizing" is like identifying the authentic seed of a beautiful flower. "Training" is like planting the seed in fertile soil, applying water, and so on — not leaving the seed lying on bare stone. The seed needs the right circumstances to grow in. By applying these skillful means, nothing whatsoever can prevent the plant from growing. Likewise, we need to train in, to develop the strength of the recognition of mind nature. After applying water and creating positive nurturing conditions, the plant will certainly grow taller and taller. Eventually, it will fully blossom with beautiful brightly colored flowers, because this potential was inherent to the seed. But this does not happen all at once. In the same way, we hear about the amazingly great qualities of buddhahood, such as the fourfold fearlessness, the eighteen unique qualities of the buddhas, the ten powers, the ten strengths and so forth. We then wonder, "Where are those qualities? How come they are not apparent in a moment's experience of the awakened state? What is wrong?" It can be understood in the following way. Within a few seconds" glimpse of the state of rigpa, these qualities are not experienced the same as when recognition has been stabilized. Although inherently present in our nature, these qualities do not have time to be fully manifest. Just as the seed is the unmistaken element for the fully blossomed flower, so the moment of recognizing the awakened state is definitely the basis for buddhahood itself.

If the flower-seed is planted and nurtured, it will without question grow. But do not expect the moment of rigpa to be an amazing or spectacular experience. Actually, there is one aspect of the awakened state that is truly amazing — the fact that conceptual thinking and the three poisons are totally absent. If we look around, apart from rigpa, what can really bring an end to thought, the very creator of samsara? We can drop a million nuclear bombs on this world and blow everything into smithereens. If that stops conceptual thinking and delusion, let's do it! But it doesn't. It would be fantastic if we could simply blow up all the confused samsaric realms and end them permanently, but unfortunately that's not possible. Is there anything in this world that stops deluded thinking? Nothing other than the moment of recognizing the awakened state can truly cut through the stream of deluded thinking. That's quite amazing. Do not expect the actual moment of rigpa to be something dramatic; but, this particular quality of it is something truly amazing!

In the past, masters like Kyungpo Naljor, Tilopa and Naropa visited Uddiyana and described the visions they had there of Vajra Yogini's pure realm, which is full of terrifying charnel grounds and frightening eternal fires and so on. More recently a group of normal people went there, and returned saying all they saw were some big boulders and a small pond of water. "We didn't see anything; it's just a normal place," they told a master named Gendün Chöpel, who died a few decades ago. In response, he said, "While you don't even see the unchanging nature of mind which is inseparable from yourself, how can you ever have visions of deities through sadhana practice?" In other words, if you are unable to see what you already continuously possess, how can you expect to perceive Vajra Yogini's pure land?

Sentient beings are never apart from this unchanging, innate nature of mind for even an instant, yet they do not see it. Just as the nature of fire is heat and the nature of water is moisture, the nature of our mind is rigpa, nondual awareness. While we are never apart from this, we still do not recognize it. How then can we expect to have any special visions? We must first be well-established in dharmata; then it is possible to see the divine city of Vajra Yogini. If we did not have the buddha nature, who could be blamed for not noticing it. But, just as water is always wet and fire is always hot, the nature of our mind is always awareness wisdom. We cannot be separated from our intrinsic nature.

Devotion and Compassion

WE ATTAIN COMPLETE ENLIGHTENMENT by unifying means and knowledge, *prajna* and *upaya*. The definitions of these two aspects varies according to the different vehicles. In the Sutra teachings, the means is compassion, while the knowledge is emptiness. By unifying compassion and emptiness, we attain true and complete enlightenment.

Tantric teachings equate the means aspect with the development stage and the knowledge aspect with the completion stage. By unifying these two stages, we attain true and complete enlightenment.

According to the Mahamudra system, the means aspect is the Six Doctrines of Naropa, while the knowledge aspect is Mahamudra practice itself. These two are called the *path of means* and the *path of liberation*. By unifying means and liberation, we attain true and complete enlightenment.

In the Madhyamika system, the Middle Way, the means aspect is relative truth; the knowledge aspect is ultimate truth. It is by unifying these two truths that we attain true and complete enlightenment.

Finally, in the Dzogchen teachings, the means aspect is called "spontaneously present nature," while the knowledge aspect is called "primordially pure essence." By unifying primordial purity and spontaneous presence, Trekchö and Tögal, we attain true and complete enlightenment.

To illustrate another aspect of all these different metaphors of union, let's use the example of an airplane. For a plane to fly through the sky requires a full assembly of the different mechanical components necessary, as well as a person capable of assembling these parts and flying the machine. If you have a skilled engineer or pilot but lack the proper parts, the airplane cannot fly. Similarly, to have all the mechanical equipment but to lack the pilot or engineer is also insufficient. It is only when the factors of means and knowledge are united that the plane can fly.

In an earlier chapter, I mentioned that buddha nature has been present in all beings since beginningless time. It is not a new thing that we achieve through effort or meditation; rather, it is something that is primordially present as our very nature. This buddha nature has never for a single instant been apart from our mind. Only due to not acknowledging it have we strayed through samsaric existence. This straying about due to the ignorance of our nature has been going on not just for a few lifetimes but since beginningless time. Until now, our nature, the enlightened essence, has been veiled in thick layers of ignorance and disturbing emotions. Now we must recognize this nature as it is, free from all obscurations. But merely recognizing our nature is not enough. We must stabilize the recognition by applying it in practice, because if we do not familiarize ourselves with our buddha nature, we will inevitably fall under the power of disturbing emotions again and again. It is said, "You may recognize your essence, but if you do not grow familiar with it, your thoughts will arise as enemies and you will be as helpless as a baby on a battlefield."

Another teaching says, "Apart from depending upon the gathering of the two accumulations and the blessings of a qualified guru, relying on other methods is delusion." The purpose of gathering the two accumulations is to purify our obscurations. And the method for realizing buddha nature requires devotion from the core of our hearts — not mere lip-service or platitudes, but a true and genuine devotion to the Three Jewels. There is a lot of talk about emptiness in Buddhism. It is considered a very important and profound subject. However unless we make it our personal experience and increasingly familiarize ourselves with it, our idea of emptiness may vary wildly from year to year, depending on our current intellectual fantasies, and we will not make much progress. So, how can we make genuine progress in our personal experience? Chiefly through devotion to the Three Jewels. The compassionate activity of the buddhas is like a hook that is just waiting to catch sentient beings who are ready and open and who are attuned to this compassion. If we have faith and devotion, we are like an iron ring that can be caught by the hook. But if we are closed and lack faith and devotion, we are like a solid iron ball. Not even the "hooks" of the buddhas can catch an iron ball.

It is not that the buddhas are without compassion or disregard certain sentient beings. Their compassion and activity are impartial and all-pervasive, like the sun shining in the sky. But if we are like a cave that faces north, the sunshine will never reach inside us. We need to have faith and devotion in order to connect with the compassionate power of the buddhas. If we do not possess these qualities, we cannot open ourselves to this connection, and there is no way that the buddhas can help us.

The state of enlightenment is totally beyond concepts. There is no joy or sorrow within it, such as being happy when one is pleased or feeling sad when one is treated badly. The state of buddhahood is beyond all these. Because of this, Buddhas make no preferences between sentient beings; each one is like their only child. The compassionate "hook" of their enlightened activity is totally impartial and all-pervasive, like the sunshine radiating from the sun.

The compassion of the awakened state is beyond both partiality and distance. It is like sunshine in that it is totally unbiased. It is not that the sun shines on some countries and not on others; The sun has no concept that "I will shine on that spot, and leave this one in darkness." The buddhas" compassion transcends all distance as well. Imagine that you have positioned a mirror facing the sun: the moment you do so, the sun's rays are instantly reflected. It is the same with the buddhas: the moment we think of them, they "gaze" on us; the rays of their compassion contact us.

The state of enlightenment lies beyond time and space. Its capacity is such that an instant as brief as a snap of the fingers can be transformed into an entire aeon, and an aeon can be transformed into a single moment. We are never excluded from the gaze of enlightened beings. We are never outside their vision. The enlightened state of all the buddhas, bodhisattvas, the dakas and dakinis and so forth is the dharmadhatu itself. This state of realization is said to be of "one taste," identical in its essential pure nature. All the various buddhas are like different butter lamps lit in one room. The individual flames are separate and distinct, but the nature of the light itself is indivisible.

The state of mind of all the buddhas is dharmakaya itself. The nature of our mind is also dharmakaya. The fact that we have the same essence serves as a direct link between us and all awakened beings. Lacking faith and devotion, it is as though the dharmakaya nature of our mind is encased in obscurations. But the very moment you open up in devotion, you receive the blessings of the buddhas.

The dharmakaya of enlightened beings is like a butter lamp where the flame is burning brightly. The dharmakaya nature of a sentient beings" mind is like a butter lamp where the wick has not yet been lit. Therefore, it is very important to allow the compassion and blessings of enlightened beings to enter us. The link between us and the state of enlightenment is faith and devotion. To simply think, "I will only worry about recognizing mind essence," while not engendering any trust in the authentic enlightened state will not help us progress very much.

To progress in the practice of recognizing mind essence, it's exceedingly important to generate faith and devotion towards enlightened beings and compassion towards those who are not enlightened. One reason for compassion is that all sentient beings, without a single exception, have been our mothers in past lives. Imagine that we could somehow roll the entire world up into small pellets and count them. The number of these pellets would still be less than the number of mothers that we have had in our past lives. Among all the six classes of sentient beings, there is not a single one who has not been our mother. This is why we always hear repeated in the teachings, "All sentient beings, my mothers, ..." or "my mother sentient beings ...." Actually, all sentient beings are our mothers from past lives.

Why is a mother so special? When we are born, we are totally helpless and incapable of caring for ourselves. We are absolutely dependent upon our mother. She is the one who looks after us much more in the beginning than our father does. A father may of course be kind, but not in the same way as a mother. A mother gives constant, unconditional love and care to a baby — she pays more attention to it than to herself. In fact, a mother is continually saving her baby's life: if she just abandoned it, it would not remain alive. An infant is that helpless.

Some people are puzzled by the nature of compassion and want to know what is meant by the term. Here's an example: imagine that your mother is in front of you, surrounded by slaughterers who chop off her hands, legs and arms. They pull out her eyes, cut off her ears and nose, and finally chop off her head. How would you feel seeing your mother chopped up into pieces? Wouldn't you feel desperately sad and grief-stricken? That emotion is compassion. Right now we may merely think of our present mother, but, in fact, all other sentient beings — no matter who they are, even animals — have been our mothers. Our present separation from them is only a matter of time and space. If we really take this to heart, how can we help not feeling compassion for all sentient beings?

All sentient beings want only happiness. No one wants to suffer. But through attachment, anger and delusion, beings only create negative karma for themselves, forging a path straight into the three lower realms. In the past, our mother sentient beings headed to these three unfortunate states; in the present moment, they are heading there again, and in the future they will continue on that same painful route. Contemplating this, how can we help but feel compassion? The emotion this evokes is what is meant by compassion. If we keep turning our backs and abandoning all our mothers for the sake of our own pleasure and benefit, thinking, "I will do a little meditation, attain enlightenment and be happy," then what kind of people are we? Isn't that a totally heartless way to behave?

Without fertile soil a seed cannot grow into a flower. Compassion is like that fertile soil. The blessing of faith is like the rain that falls from above. When the seed of training in mind essence is planted in the fertile soil of compassion and is watered by the rain of blessings through our devotion, it will automatically grow.

A genuinely compassionate person is naturally honest and decent, and will shy away from hurting others through evil deeds. Therefore, he or she will automatically progress and will engender many qualities. If we have compassion, we will naturally heed the cause and effect of our actions. We will be careful. Someone who lacks compassion can easily become a complete charlatan who does not care about anyone else. Such an impostor only takes advantage of others. He or she will definitely not progress.

To lack trust in enlightened beings is like planting a seed in dry soil. How will the seed grow? However, if the seed meets with fertile soil and rainwater, nothing can prevent it from sprouting and growing. Conversely, the seed lying on bare rock without fertile soil and moisture will remain the same from year to year, with no difference, no progress.

It is not enough to practice by merely sitting and saying, "Empty, empty. This mind is empty!" We want to genuinely progress: in order to do this, faith and devotion are essential, and compassion is indispensable. Without devotion and compassion, we are as hardened as someone who sees a buddha fly past in the sky and says, "So what!" Or we are like someone who watches another living creature being chopped up with their entrails hanging out who says, "I don't care!" Then our practice is no different from the seed lying on bare stone. It will never grow. When such a jaded and faithless person sees the buddhas fly by in the sky, he thinks, "They are probably just holding their breath or pulling some trick." Likewise, when he sees another person being cut up, he says, "That's their karma. It has nothing to do with me. I'm fine here. Their suffering is their business." With such an attitude there will never be any true progress in meditation.

Here is another example for someone who lacks faith. Let's say that we tell them about how the American lifestyle is, about the beautiful houses and gadgets and so forth. That other person might reply, "I don't believe you. I've never been there and seen them, so these things cannot exist. You're lying: whatever I haven't seen doesn't exist." This may sound absurd, but many, many people have said, "I don't see any buddhafields, so they don't exist. I don't see any hell realms, so there are no such places."

The reason I do not think this way is that I trust in my main teacher, Buddha Shakyamuni. He could clearly perceive the three times and see the six realms of sentient beings and all the buddhafields in every direction. Because of the depth and profundity of his wisdom, I consider everything he said to be utterly and flawlessly true. Between Buddha Shakyamuni and myself there has been a lineage of great masters in whom I also have total trust. This trust extends all the way to my root guru, in whom I have complete faith from the very core of my heart. I have total confidence in all these beings; I don't feel that any one of them ever told a lie.

Since Buddha Shakyamuni there have been countless other practitioners who have had that same trust and confidence in the teachings of the enlightened ones. Through these qualities they were able to attain great accomplishment. They could fly through the sky, pass through solid matter and reach complete enlightenment in a single lifetime. If we disbelieve the statements of the buddhas because we can't experience such things through our own senses, we are like someone who, when he is told, "Behind this hill are some villages," replies "No there aren't, because I haven't seen them." How does that sound? Doesn't it sound stupid?

These many practitioners of the past trusted the Buddha when he said, "There are buddhafields above and lower realms below; in between are the effects of our own karmic actions." They had confidence in the words of the enlightened one, the statements of the bodhisattvas, and in the oral instructions of their own root gurus. Inspired by this trust, they put the teachings into practice, and through doing so they gained realization. In fact, they could not avoid attaining accomplishment; neither could they avoid benefiting countless other beings. This is not merely an old story from the past; this is still happening today.

If we rely only on our own personal and limited experience as the measure for everything, we can certainly say, "I don't see any buddhafields, so there aren't any. I don't see any hell realms below, so there aren't any. If I do something negative right now, I don't suddenly end up in the lower realms. Nothing at all happens. Therefore, my actions have no effect." But fortunately we have more than our own limited knowledge to rely on when we evaluate such statements. We have the words of the perfectly enlightened one, as well as the lineage of great masters. There have been and indeed still are countless practitioners who have been able to attain accomplishment through their trust in the buddhas. This is the reason we *can* feel complete trust in those teachings.

I myself have never been to any buddhafields with this present body, so I could say that according to my own experience there are no buddhafields. Similarly, in this very body, I have never been to the hells, so I could say that there are none. I could also say that my actions have no karmic consequences. I could certainly be in doubt about all these things, were it not for the three types of perfect measure. These are the words of the Buddha, the statements of the great bodhisattvas and the oral instructions of our own root gurus. For these reasons I myself can say I do not have any doubt regarding these matters, but totally trust in these teachings. This kind of trust makes accomplishment through Dharma practice possible. Conversely, if we continue to hesitate and generate doubts about the teachings of the Buddha, accomplishment is not possible.

Take this example: in one hand I have a huge diamond, in the other a chunk of glass. I say, "One of these is a diamond: would you like to buy it for a very good price?" Now, you are not sure which is the diamond and which is just glass. Because of this doubt, you would have to say, "I don't know," and you would never be able to purchase the diamond no matter how much of a bargain it would be. That is how it is to be in doubt. Doubt hampers every activity we do in this world, no matter what.

To sum up, we need devotion to enlightened beings and compassion to those who are not. Possessing these two, what is then the main training? It is maintaining nondistraction. When we forget mind essence and are carried away, the demon of distraction lies in ambush. But with devotion and compassion, the practice of recognizing mind essence will automatically progress. Many people come to me saying, "I've tried to meditate for years, but nothing happens; I'm not making any progress." This is because of not using the effective method, the right means. We may have the knowledge aspect of having recognized mind essence, but without combining it with means of trust and compassion, we will not make any headway. We may know how to assemble and drive a car, but if we do not have the necessary parts we will never be able to ride anywhere.

Please keep this teaching at the very core of your heart; not at the edge or to one side of your heart, but at the very center. Please think, "That old Tibetan man said devotion and compassion are essential. I'll keep that right in the center of my heart." I have wanted to say this for a long time, but I feel that now people are more willing to listen. It's because it's extremely important that I felt it should be said.

I am telling you the truth here. I am being honest with you. I am not lying. If you practice the way I have described here, then each month and year will yield progress. And in the end, no one will be able to pull you back or prevent you from attaining enlightenment.

THE QUALIFIED MASTER

BEFORE SETTING OUT ON THE PATH of liberation and enlightenment, we need to meet a true qualified master. To find such a person we must first understand the characteristics that exemplify such an individual. When we go to school we need a good teacher. If your teacher is a complete moron without any skill, how can you learn anything from him? In the same way, the kind of spiritual teacher we are looking for is a person who can guide us all the way to liberation and the omniscient state of enlightenment. Isn't that true?

"Liberation" means taking rebirth in a pure buddhafield after this life. The "omniscient state of enlightenment" is complete buddhahood endowed with all perfect qualities and totally free from any defects whatsoever. We should be seeking the kind of teacher who can surely lead us to that state. The most qualified teacher is called a "vajra-holder possessing the three precepts." He or she should possess the perfect qualities of being outwardly endowed with the vows of individual liberation, called *pratimoksha,* while inwardly possessing the trainings of a bodhisattva. On the innermost level, the qualified master must be competent in the true state of samadhi.

A person who possesses only the vows of individual liberation that correspond to Hinayana practice, is called a "virtuous guide." If a person in addition possesses the bodhisattva trainings, he or she is called a "spiritual teacher." If a person is adept in the Vajrayana practices along with these vows and trainings, he or she is called a *dorje lobpön,* or "vajra master."

A true vajra master should have already liberated his own stream-of-being through realization. This means actualizing the authentic state of samadhi. Furthermore, he or she should be able to liberate others through compassion and loving kindness; that is a second essential quality.

To illustrate some characteristics of a qualified vajra master I will tell you about my teacher. My guru was my uncle, Samten Gyatso. Samten Gyatso was my father's older brother and was the fourth incarnation of Ngawang Trinley. The first Ngawang Trinley was one of three brothers; the others were called Sönam Yeshe and Namgyal Tulku. These three became known as the "three wishfulfilling sons." In his succeeding lives, Ngawang Trinley's incarnation was known under the same name, Ngaktrin, depending upon where he was born; thus, Argey Ngaktrin, Tersey Ngaktrin and then Tsangsar Ngaktrin. This fourth incarnation from the Tsangsar bloodline was my uncle. I feel a little shy telling this story because there is no way I can avoid praising this person. I really don't want it to sound as if I'm indirectly praising myself by lauding a family member. However, there is a crude example I can use to illustrate this. My guru was excellent, and I am related to him, in the same way that excrement is akin to the very good food it initially was. Understand the analogy. I am just being honest. Even though I'm telling the truth, it's embarrassing because I must praise someone of my own lineage.

Samten Gyatso's background, both in family line and Dharma lineage, was Barom Kagyü. This lineage originated with a master named Barom Dharma Wangchuk, one of the chief disciples of Gampopa. Gampopa's guru was Milarepa. Milarepa's guru was Marpa, the Translator. Marpa's guru was Naropa. Naropa's guru was Tilopa. Tilopa's guru was Vajradhara. That was tracing the lineage upwards. Now, tracing the line back down, Barom Dharma Wangchuk had a disciple named Tishi Repa. Tishi Repa's disciple was Sangwa Repa Karpo, whose disciple was, in turn, Tsangsar Lümey Dorje who was my family ancestor. His chief disciple was Tsangsar Jangchub Shönnu, who was his nephew.

The Barom Kagyü lineage was passed on from father to son through ten generations all the way down to Tsangsar Lhatsün who attained rainbow body. These men were the kings of the country of Nangchen. In addition, they held political and religious positions, called *Tishi, Pakshi* or *Gushi,* assigned to them by the Chinese emperor. When the Nangchen kingdom was eventually divided into two, my family gave up their right to the throne and became *ngakpas* wearing white skirts and shawls. The bloodline continued, but the family members were no longer kings of the country. During this time, what we now call Greater Tibet was divided into the several regions that include Central Tibet and the eastern kingdoms of Derge and Nangchen. After Tsangsar Lhatsün attained rainbow body, seven more generations followed until my father.

I am not bringing this up as a way to brag about having a special background, only to explain that the teaching and family lineage were one. As I mentioned before, my uncle, my root guru, was from the Tsangsar family line. Samten Gyatso's mother, Könchok Paldrön, was the daughter of the tertön Chokgyur Lingpa. Samten Gyatso held as well that lineage known as Chokling Tersar, the New Treasures of Chokgyur Lingpa.

Within the Barom Kagyü lineage, Samten Gyatso was regarded as an emanation of four-armed Mahakala. The second incarnation of Chokgyur Lingpa once had a pure vision of Samten Gyatso in which he saw him as an emanation of Vimalamitra. Externally, Samten Gyatso kept the Vinaya very purely and strictly. In his entire life, he never tasted alcohol nor ate any meat. Inwardly, in tune with the bodhisattva trainings, he always kept a low profile. He never dressed up; instead he wore the robes of an ordinary monk. He was never adorned with anything special, such as brocade.

People said he had a very high view or realization, but he did not talk about it. Once though, he told me, "At a young age I was introduced to mind essence. Since then until now, I have not had any great problems at all in sustaining the view; as a matter of fact, there does not seem to be any difference between day and night." To repeat, a "vajra-holder possessing the three levels of precepts" holds the external precepts, that are the moral disciplines of individual liberation. He also holds the internal precepts, that are the bodhisattva trainings, and the innermost Vajrayana precepts called samaya. Samten Gyatso had perfected all three.

His gurus were Karma Khenpo, Rinchen Dargye, Chokgyur Lingpa's son, Tsewang Norbu, and the 15th Karmapa, Khakyab Dorje. Besides them, Samten Gyatso received teachings from many other masters. Later on, the transmission of the Chokling Tersar that most of the great lamas of those days received came through Samten Gyatso.

He offered the transmission of the entire Chokling Tersar to the 15th Karmapa, to Drukchen Rinpoche, the head of the Drukpa Kagyü School, and to Taklung Tsetrül Rinpoche, at the main seat of the Taklung Kagyü School in central Tibet. Samten Gyatso was also invited to Tsechu Monastery in Nangchen, the foremost monastery in the kingdom. There he gave the transmission of the Chokling Tersar to the king of Nangchen and thereby became one of the king's gurus.

At one time, Samten Gyatso was invited to Palpung Monastery, one of the chief monasteries in the Derge kingdom, which was headed by Situ Wangchok Gyalpo, the predecessor of the present-day Situ Rinpoche. He transmitted part of the Chokling Tersar to Situ Wangchok Gyalpo and was therefore counted as one of Situ Rinpoche's gurus.

Dzongsar Khyentse, the reincarnation of Jamyang Khyentse Wangpo, came to Samten Gyatso's mountain top hermitage of Randza Dzong-go. There Dzongsar Khyentse requested the transmission of the sections of the Chokling Tersar composed by the 15th Karmapa, Khakyab Dorje, that he had not received.

It is said that the confidence of the Dharma influences other people's experience. Because of possessing this courage Samten Gyatso was never afraid of anyone. He always wore ordinary simple clothing. He never dressed in a special fashion, no matter who came to see him or whom he went to meet, even though he encountered some of the highest masters of Tibet. Although he never put on any conspicuous finery, when he entered a room people always made way for him. Even if they were important dignitaries, people were completely terrified of him. They would immediately move to the side to make a path for him to walk.

Even the Karmapa was a little afraid of Samten Gyatso. He once told a companion, "I'm really terrified of that lama. I don't know why, but he really scares me." Even I would have to tell myself, "I don't have to be afraid; after all, he's my uncle!" Yet every morning when I stood before the door to my uncle's quarters, I would always hesitate and think twice before daring to open the door. There was nothing to really be afraid of, but everyone, including me, was somehow intimidated by Samten Gyatso. He possessed some remarkable quality, an intensely commanding presence.

One of Samten Gyatso's gurus, Karmey Khenpo Rinchen Dargye, was reborn as the son of Samten Gyatso's sister. He was called Khentrül, meaning the incarnation of Karmey Khenpo. This young incarnation once said to me, "Why should we be scared of him: Samten Gyatso is our uncle." The young Khentrül was quite courageous, and eloquent in a remarkable way. However, whenever he came into Samten Gyatso's presence and saw his bald head Khentrül would forget what he was about to say. He would lower his gaze and start to tremble very slightly.

Since he was guru to the king, Samten Gyatso was often summoned to the palace, where he would preside over the various religious ceremonies. He would stay in the old palace, while the king and his family resided in the new palace. In the new palace was an assembly hall called the Square Hall, where the big chieftains, ministers and dignitaries sat with their haughty airs. The king, who was quite eccentric, would not allow any upholstered seating in this room — only hard wooden benches. No matter how special the ministers might be, they had to sit on bare wooden planks. Nevertheless, they sat there in their fine brocade *chubas* with long sleeves. When they strutted about, they kept their noses in the air and did not pay any attention to ordinary people.

When Samten Gyatso came to see the royal family each morning, he had to pass through this hall. He would often cough slightly before entering. When the dignitaries heard the "cough" approaching, they would all try to stand up at once. Sometimes they tried to stand up by leaning on the shoulder of the person next to them. Then, because they were all using the same support system, they would all tumble here and there and make a mess of themselves. They were all completely terrified of Samten Gyatso.

I was often one of the two attendants who accompanied Samten Gyatso on his visits to the living-quarters of the royal family. When Samten Gyatso entered their room, the queen prince and princesses would all immediately abandon whatever they were doing and leap to their feet. The king himself had long before turned over his rule to the prince and was seldom seen because he remained in meditation retreat.

Samten Gyatso never flattered others by playing up to them or telling them how wonderful they were. He spoke in a very straightforward manner. If something was true, he would say it was; if it was not, he would say it was not — without adding or subtracting anything. He never talked around the subject. If anyone started to speak to him directly concerning his amazing qualities, he would not allow them an opening. For instance, if they began to say, "Rinpoche, you are very learned ..." or "You must be very realized ..." he would scold them immediately. He never tolerated that.

Samten Gyatso kept to the "hidden yogi style" whereby he did not show his accomplishments to anyone, and definitely did not behave as if he was someone special. He never blessed people by placing his hand on their heads, he did not permit others to prostrate to him and he never sat on a high seat. He spent most of his early life living in caves. If he had any understanding or special powers, he did not ever show them to anyone. He did not build temples or erect statues. During the first part of his life, he always had four or five private scribes with him. He had the entire Chokling Tersar, almost 40 volumes, copied out. In fact, this is the only thing he actually put any effort into, having the whole Chokling Tersar written down exactly.

How then was Samten Gyatso installed as a vajra master? It happened in the following way. The 15th Karmapa had wanted to receive the transmission of the Chokling Tersar from Chokgyur Lingpa's son, Tsewang Norbu. At that time, Tsewang Norbu had arrived in Central Tibet and was staying in Lhasa at a benefactor's home. Khakyab Dorje sent for him and Tsewang Norbu agreed to go. Unfortunately his self-important benefactor, not wanting to let go of his resident priest, made it difficult for Tsewang Norbu to leave. Tsewang Norbu died soon after without ever having the chance to travel to Tsurphu and transmit the Chokling Tersar.

Karmapa then sent for Tsewang Norbu's nephew, Tersey Tulku. He was a reincarnation of Tsewang Norbu's brother, another son of Chokgyur Lingpa who died while still very young and was eventually reborn as the son of Chokgyur Lingpa's daughter, Könchok Paldrön. He was the youngest of her four sons, being my uncle and the brother of Samten Gyatso. Tersey Tulku was extremely learned and paid great attention to details. He was totally qualified to give the Chokling Tersar in a very precise way. After he arrived in Central Tibet, the Karmapa sent him a message, to come to Tsurphu.

Karmapa sent Tersey Tulku his most trusted servant, a monk from the Golok province named Jampal Tsültrim, to make this request. Jampal Tsültrim was of very good stock and character. Though he served as Karmapa's servant, he was a master in his own right. He was the Karmapa's scribe and a very pure monk. He was a very impressive and reliable personage, so the Karmapa sent him on this mission. However, since he was from Golok, he was quite tough-minded and extremely self-assured. When he visited Tersey Tulku, he told him, "The Karmapa requests that you come and give him the Chokling Tersar." Tersey Tulku was, like his brother Samten Gyatso, a hidden yogi type, so he refused outright, saying, "This is utterly ridiculous! How can a dog put his paw on a man's head? Why are you making this demand?" Gelong Jampal Tsültrim said, "I'm not asking you to do this; it's the Karmapa giving you the command. Do you want to break samaya with him?" Tersey Tulku said, "No, he's a bodhisattva on the tenth bhumi. I'm the same as a dog. I'm nothing. How can I act as his guru, giving him empowerments? There is absolutely no question about this — how can I do it?" Then they got into a heated argument and Gelong Jampal Tsültrim finally slapped him across the face and said, "You lowlife!" He then walked away. He returned to Khakyab Dorje and said, "This man is impossible — the lowest of the low! I argued with him, but he totally refuses to come." The 15th Karmapa was not upset about this. He merely said, "That's all right. We'll see. Maybe it will work out in the end."

Khakyab Dorje then invited Samten Gyatso to come to Tsurphu, but he didn't tell him exactly what the purpose of the visit was supposed to be.

Sometime after Samten Gyatso had arrived at Tsurphu, he was invited to come to Khakyab Dorje's private chambers. When he got there, he saw a throne set out with brocade robes, a crown and all the paraphernalia of a vajra master. He was told to sit on the throne. At first there was much protesting back and forth, but finally Khakyab Dorje said, "I command you to sit there. From now on, I install you in the position of vajra master."

It was not only the Karmapa who forced the role of vajra master on Samten Gyatso; Tsewang Norbu did so as well. Tsewang Norbu was once invited to Riwoche to give the *Rinchen Terdzö* empowerments. Since Chokgyur Lingpa had already passed away, they wanted to receive this cycle from, at best, Jamgön Kongtrül, but he was quite elderly and weak. Next best, they wanted Khyentse, but he was too old. Then both Khyentse and Kongtrül decided to send the son of Chokgyur Lingpa, Tsewang Norbu, as their representative to give the *Rinchen Terdzö*. Many great tulkus were present there, including the two reincarnations of Chokgyur Lingpa.

Each evening after the ceremonies, the tulkus and great lamas would gather in Tsewang Norbu's private room for discussions and question and answer sessions. One night, they were discussing the future of the Chokling Tersar. Tsewang Norbu was a very large man, with a commanding presence and piercing eyes. He just glared at them. Then he pointed his finger at Samten Gyatso, who had been sitting silently near the door keeping a low profile. Tsewang Norbu said, looking at Tersey Tulku [Tersey means the son of the tertön], "You think that you are the incarnation of Chokgyur Lingpa's son!" Looking at the two Chokling tulkus he said; "You two think you are incarnations of Chokgyur Lingpa himself. All three of you think you are someone very special! But you aren't compared to that one over there!" Pointing to Samten Gyatso, he continued, "He will be much more influential in maintaining the lineage." Samten Gyatso was very frightened by this statement. Although Tsewang Norbu was his maternal uncle, everyone was a little afraid of him. When he made a statement like this, it was like a prophecy that really sunk in.

When Tsewang Norbu left for Central Tibet many years later, he seemed to know he would never meet Samten Gyatso again. He enthroned Samten Gyatso privately in his chambers and, giving him his vajra and bell, Tsewang Norbu said, "I entrust you with the lineage of the Chokling Tersar. You will have to pass it on in the future." Although Samten Gyatso protested, he was still invested with this responsibility. That's why he didn't refuse later on when Khakyab Dorje invited him to come to Tsurphu. He said, "All right," and he gave the empowerments.

When Samten Gyatso was giving Khakyab Dorje the entire transmission of the Chokling Tersar, Khakyab Dorje was not staying at Tsurphu proper, but remained in his retreat place above Tsurphu. He was elderly at this time. He had recently remarried and his consort was called Khandro Chenmo, meaning the Great Dakini of the Karmapa. She was only about sixteen years old then; the Karmapa died three years later when she was 19. Tersey Tulku was also there at that time. He was no longer shy about coming to Tsurphu once his brother had agreed to give the empowerments. In the evenings they would often talk with Khakyab Dorje, sometimes until midnight or later. Khakyab Dorje would then leave Samten Gyatso's retreat hut and return to his quarters. One night, after they had parted, Khakyab Dorje joined his palms and told his consort, "At this time and during this age, probably no one except Samten Gyatso has authentic realization of the innermost essence of the Great Perfection." That was the kind of pure appreciation the Karmapa had for Samten Gyatso. The Great Dakini herself told this to me later.

To be established in the role of a vajra master can be a bit problematic. In the case of Samten Gyatso he was forcefully installed in that position by Tsewang Norbu, his root guru, and by Khakyab Dorje. Samten Gyatso never said much about this to anyone. Shortly before Samten Gyatso died, I spent many evenings in his room. Samten Gyatso would lie in his bed and I would sleep at his feet on the floor near him. One night we were talking, and Samten Gyatso began to speak for the first time about his innermost realization. He also told the details I've just related above about his relationship with Khakyab Dorje, Tsewang Norbu and so forth. Apart from this time he never related this personal information to anyone.

"From that point on," he told me, "I really fell under the power of one of the four Maras, the demon of distraction called the "heavenly son." Before that, my only ambition was to remain in a cave and do practice. But since Karmapa forced me into this, I now have to behave like a vajra master and give empowerments, reading transmissions, etc." This is something he had never done before. He had always side-stepped it completely. But from then on, he had to undertake that position. When looking back, there is now no doubt that he became the one responsible for widely propagating the Chokling Tersar teachings.

Samten Gyatso himself said: "I was happy just to live in caves. I never had the intention or desire to act like a lama. At the age of eight I was introduced to mind nature, and I have remained in it as much as possible till this time." So when Samten Gyatso grew older, he often thought, "I should have stayed in caves; instead, I fell under the power of hindrances." It was not empty talk when he said this; he actually did feel that way. He had no ambition to become a vajra master or sit above anyone else. He once told me, "Being successful is actually called the "pleasant obstacle." While unpleasant obstacles are easily recognized by everyone, the pleasant obstacle is rarely acknowledged to be an obstacle." Unpleasant obstacles are, for example, being defamed or implicated in scandals, falling sick, meeting with misfortune and so forth. Most practitioners can deal with these. They recognize these situations as obstacles and use them as part of the path. But pleasant obstacles, such as becoming renowned, collecting a following of disciples, and superficially acting for the welfare of others, are much more deceptive. One starts to think, "My goodness! I'm becoming really special. I'm benefiting many beings. Everything is perfectly fine!" One does not readily notice that one is falling prey to pleasant obstacles, and this is why they are a major hindrance for progress. Samten Gyatso warned that people rarely recognize these hindrances. They usually only think, "My capacity for benefiting others is expanding!" Well, this is what one tells oneself while failing to notice that one has fallen prey to an obstacle.

MINDFULNESS

THERE ARE THE TWO TYPES OF MINDFULNESS: deliberate and effortless. By starting out with the mindfulness of deliberate attention, the practitioner can make a clear distinction between being distracted or not. Effortless mindfulness is of course possible if you happen to be one of the people of the highest caliber — the instantaneous type of person — who does not really need to go through the path. However, for most other people, especially in the Mahamudra system, the mindfulness of deliberate attention is essential in the beginning. Otherwise, by relying on only effortless mindfulness, you may not even notice whether you are distracted or not. Even worse, you may convince yourself that you are never distracted. Rather than this, it is much better to practice deliberate mindfulness even though it is subtly conceptual, and gradually progress to effortless mindfulness.

In the Mahamudra teachings, you often find the phrase "original innate nature." This is none other than buddha nature. The training is simply to become used to that, whether you call it Mahamudra, Madhyamika or Dzogchen. These are all different words for the same natural state. But to train, you must first of all be introduced to and have recognized the view. In Mahamudra, once the practitioner has recognized the view, he or she takes mindfulness as the path; it is a way of training in that view. If mindfulness is lost, then we are led completely astray into the "black dissipation" of ordinary habitual patterns. Black dissipation means that one forgets all thought of practice and simply deviates into ordinary activities. All practice is left behind. So, either we remember the view and sustain it, or the practice is destroyed. We need to know when we are distracted.

Discursive thought is distraction, but once we recognize the essence of the thought; we have arrived at nonthought. A quote from *The Rain of Wisdom* by Jamgön Lodrö Thaye says: "Within complexity I discovered dharmakaya; within thought I discovered nonthought."

A person of the highest capacity can immediately arrive at effortless mindfulness. This is someone who possesses the continuity of former training from the life before this, who is reborn with a very strong aptitude for this type of practice. Needless to say, most people do not belong to that category. Most of us are not of the highest capacity, so there is no way around having to remind ourselves of the view by deliberately being mindful.

We need an intentional reminder to bring us back to the view. That which goes astray is simply our attention. Our mind becomes distracted, and that which brings us back to the view is called "deliberate mindfulness." In the same way, if you want the light to come on in a room, a conscious act is necessary. You must put your finger on the light-switch and press it; the light doesn't turn itself on. In the same way, unless a beginner reminds him or herself determinedly to remember the view, the recognition of mind essence never occurs. The moment we notice that we are carried away, we think, "I have wandered off." By recognizing the identity of who has been distracted, you have automatically arrived back in the view. The reminder is nothing more than that. This moment is like pressing the light-switch. Once the light is on, you do not have to keep on pressing it. After a while, we again forget and are carried away. At that point, we must reapply deliberate mindfulness.

This case is a good example for the famous phrase, "The artificial leads to the natural." First apply the method; then, once you are in the natural state; simply allow its continuity. Of course, after a while our attention begins to wander again. We may not even notice the distraction; it is as subtle and sneaky as a thief. But having noticed the distraction, apply mindfulness and remain naturally. That natural state is effortless mindfulness.

What is important here is a sense of natural ongoingness or continuity. Strike a bell, and the sound will continue for some time. In the same way, by deliberate mindfulness you recognize the essence, and that recognition lasts for some time. As it is unnecessary to continually press the light switch in a lit room, likewise, you do not have to keep on striking the bell to make the sound last. When recognizing mind essence, you simply let be. Simply leave it as it is, and it will last for a short while. This is called "sustaining the continuity." Nonfabrication means not to stray from this continuity.

Our main obstacle to practice is being distracted. The very moment you recognize mind essence, it is seen that there is no thing to see. There is no act of meditating at that point; it is seen in the moment of looking. When recognizing, simply leave it, without tampering with or modifying it in any way: this is called nonfabrication. Once that continuity is lost, we are distracted, carried away. There is no distraction within the continuity; distraction is impossible. Losing the continuity is the same as being distracted, which actually means forgetting. A trained practitioner will notice that the view has been lost. The very moment of perceiving, "I lost the view; I was carried away," recognize again, and you will immediately see emptiness. At that point leave it as it is. You do not have to have anxiety or fear about this; these are only more thoughts. From where did the thought come? It is none other than the expression of awareness. Awareness is emptiness; its expression is thought.

The Kagyü teachings say, "In the beginning, thoughts are like snowflakes falling on the surface of a lake." The lake is a body of water. The snowflakes are also water. When they meet, they mingle indivisibly. In the recognition of mind nature, the thought has no power to stand on its own. It simply vanishes. Just as our nature is emptiness, so is the nature of the thought. The moment of recognizing the thinker as empty cognizance is like the snowflake meeting the water.

This is certainly different from the thought process of an ordinary person, which is actively involved in either anger, desire or dullness. These kinds of thoughts are like etching in stone. A karmic trace is left behind. Thought activity in a yogi's mind, on the other hand, is like writing on the surface of water. The thought arises; the essence is recognized; the thought dissolves. We cannot totally eliminate our thoughts right away. However, after repeatedly recognizing the essence, thoughts will gradually diminish.

The essence itself is totally free of conceptual thinking. Yet, at the same time, its expression *is* conceptual thinking. Do not focus your attention on the expression. Rather, recognize the essence: then the expression has no power to remain anywhere. At this point, the expression simply collapses or folds back into the essence. As we become more stable in recognizing the essence free from conceptual thinking, its expression as conceptual thinking becomes increasingly baseless or unfounded. As conceptual thinking diminishes and finally vanishes, what is left to cause us to wander in samsara? The very basis for samsaric existence is none other than conceptual thinking.

In the face of directly seeing emptiness, the thought cannot remain just as no object can remain in mid-air. When we do not recognize emptiness, we are carried away continuously by thoughts. One thought after another is how the mind of sentient beings works, day and night. From beginningless lifetimes until now, thoughts have incessantly followed one another, like beads on a string. Yet the essence of each of these thoughts is emptiness, if we could only recognize it.

Repeatedly, you hear, "Recognize mind essence; attain stability in that." What this really means is that we should repeatedly look into what thinks. We should recognize the absence or emptiness of this thinker over and over again, until finally the power of deluded thinking weakens, until it is totally gone without a trace. At that point, what remains to prevent the state of enlightenment?

Buddha nature is something we already possess. It is not a product of meditation practice; nor is it something we need to accumulate or achieve. However, unless we recognize it, we gain no benefit whatsoever from possessing it. All of our thoughts come out of the buddha nature as its expression, like rays of sunlight emanate from the sun. It is not that the sun comes out of the rays. That's why, in the beginning, you should look into mind essence until you have clearly "established the natural state." Once the natural state is established, there is no point in looking here or there. It does not make any difference any longer. At that level there is an inherent stability in emptiness. Nowhere on the face of this earth, nowhere under the heavens, can you find a more effective training for attaining buddhahood. If there were a better path existing somewhere, you could at least search for it. But as it's said, "Scan the entire universe. You will not find a path superior to this." Even if you were to examine every single thing in the universe, you would not find a better method. So, train in exactly this.

It does not really matter whether we call our practice Mahamudra or Dzogchen. What is more important is that the remembering to recognize and the act of recognizing should be simultaneous, without the slightest time lapse between the two. We do not have to dance around after we remember to recognize and then sit down and recognize. We do not have to make a show out of it. We do not have to first turn right, then turn left, then look up and then down and *then* recognize. The very moment you look, it is immediately seen that there is no "thing" to see. It is seen in the moment of looking. In the moment of seeing, it is free from thought. Isn't it much less hassle to practice something this simple? This is also called *prajnaparamita,* transcendent knowledge, because it is beyond or on the "other side" of a conceptual frame of mind. This transcendent knowledge is not lying around a little out of the way, so that we need to look slightly more to the left, or a little more to the right or a little deeper inside. If it were like that, it would be difficult to recognize because we could somehow miss it.

When you point at space, do you point first and *then* reach space, or do you contact space the moment you point? Is there anything between your finger and space? When I ask this, I am not talking about the blue-colored daytime sky. I am talking about actually touching space. Understand this example: this is exactly what is meant by, "It is seen in the moment of looking. It is free in the moment of seeing." The first moment of looking into mind essence is called the "mindfulness of deliberate attention." The second moment, described as "free in the moment of seeing," does not mean one should look more, thinking, "Now, where is it? I had better look closer!" That creates more thinking. If you continue with, "Now, I see it! Where is it! I want to see it!" In this case you are just creating more thoughts within the state of buddha nature, a state that is by itself free from thought.

The first point is deliberate mindfulness. Then in the next moment of seeing your nature; you should allow for an ongoing state of naturalness. All the different speculations we can go through, such as, "I see it. I don't see it. This is the real thing! This is not really it!" should be dropped completely. They are all irrelevant thoughts. In the moment of seeing allow for a continuity free from thought. Simply rest freely in that.

Because we have been carried away from this state by conceptual thinking since beginningless lifetimes, we will again be swept away by the strength of habit. When this happens, you must notice, "I am distracted." People who have never received a teaching like this never even understand that they are being carried away. But someone who has received this teaching, and who has seen that there is no "thing" to see, will also notice when their attention wanders away from this. They can recognize distraction. Then they can look into "*Who* is being carried away?" That immediately brings about the meeting with buddha nature. At that moment, leave it as it is.

When we grow used to this practice, we can discard such thoughts as: "I need to be undistracted," or "I need to remember," or "Now I remember. Now I forgot." As stability in effortless mindfulness increases, these ideas are slowly relinquished.

Here is how the nature of mind is introduced in the Mahamudra system. First the practitioner is told, "Look into your mind." The big question at this point is, "What is mind?" The teacher will say, "Do you sometimes feel happy or sad? Do you want things? Do you like and dislike this and that? Okay, look into that which feels those emotions." After doing that, the practitioner then reports, "Well, that which thinks and feels does not seem to be a real thing. But, at the same time, there are thoughts and emotions." The teacher will say, "All right. Keep a close eye on that thinker." Afterwards, the student will return and tell the teacher, "Well, I've been looking into the thinker and sometimes it makes many thoughts about this and that and sometimes it just rests without thinking anything."

For a diligent person to reach this point in the process takes about two or three months. The disciple becomes very clear about the fact that, mind, the thinker, is not a real thing. Even though this is true, it gets involved in thinking up all possible things and sometimes remains without thinking of anything. These two states, thought-occurrence and stillness, refer to thinking and the cessation of thinking. These aspects can correspondingly be called "arising and ceasing." Through all our lifetimes since beginningless time until now, we have been caught up in the arising and ceasing of thoughts.

The teacher will then say, "Let's give these two states names. When there is thinking taking place, call it "occurrence." When there are no thoughts, call it "stillness."" This is pointing out occurrence and stillness. Normal people do not notice these two states. They do not know the difference between occurrence and stillness. After this, the disciple will feel, "Now, I understand these two states. Thinking of this and that is called occurrence. Not thinking of anything is called stillness."

The teacher will say, "Your mind is like a person who doesn't work all the time. At times he takes a rest. Sometimes he moves around and other times he sits still and doesn't do anything. Although the mind is empty, it neither works nor remains quiet all the time."

Being able to notice its thought-occurrence and stillness doesn't mean one knows the real nature of this mind. It is simply the ability to detect when there are thoughts and when there is not the presence and absence of thought. This is called "knowing the character of the mind." It is not knowing buddha nature. Sometimes your attention keeps still and sometimes it moves around. As long as you merely keep an eye on whether there is thinking or stillness and never go beyond this exercise, you will not reach enlightenment.

The teacher will then give the next instruction, saying, "Now, don't just notice whether there is stillness or thought occurrence. When there is thinking, look into the thinker. When there is stillness, look into what feels the stillness."

The disciple will return entirely bewildered and say, "When I look into what feels the stillness, I don't find anything whatsoever. When the thinking occurs and I look into what thinks, I don't find any "thing" either. Not only that, but both the thinking and the feeling of stillness disappear. Now what am I supposed to do? Before, I could take charge of something. I could identify the thinking and the stillness. But it's not like that anymore. When I look into what thinks, the thinker vanishes. When I look into what is still, that's also gone. I'm at a complete loss. I have lost both the thinker and that which feels still."

The teacher will reply, "No, you are not at all at a complete loss. Now you have arrived at Mahamudra, at the nature of mind. You need to train in this for months and years. Before, you were only concerned with the manifestation, not with the nature. Now the manifestation has vanished. What is left is the nature itself." That is the traditional way of pointing out Mahamudra.

Training in this fashion, there is no difference whatsoever between Mahamudra and Dzogchen practice. That is why so many great masters of the past have praised the Mahamudra system so highly. It is perfect for both a beginner of little capacity and for a person of great capacity. In Mahamudra there are no errors or sidetracks whatsoever.

What we should really look into from now on is that which thinks when we think and that which feels still when we are quiet. All practices prior to this point are externalized, in that one watches what occurs as an object of the attention, "Now I'm thinking. Now I'm feeling still." In both these cases, the object of attention is externalized from oneself, from the one who watches. So, from this point on we internalize the practice by *recognizing* that which thinks or that which feels still, rather than observing the feeling of it.

How can we practice this diligently, without being carried away by distraction? We must notice when we are carried away and look into *what* is being carried away. Make a very clear distinction between being and not being distracted. It is possible to convince ourselves that we are not distracted, saying, "My attention never wanders. I never get carried away."

If we are stuck in that kind of conviction, we have gone astray. This situation is very difficult to cure; it is a severe sidetrack. The very moment of recognizing mind nature and seeing no thing is itself nondistraction. But to think, "I am undistracted" is a fabrication just like any other thought.

It is easy for people to decide that mind is emptiness, but there is a difference between experiencing the real emptiness and experiencing the *idea* of emptiness, which is simply another thought. The essence of mind is primordially emptiness — there is no question about that. It is not composed of any material substance whatsoever. But when we try to articulate that, thinking, "It's empty. I see it!" then it becomes not empty. We understand that the master said, "Recognize your mind essence. See that there is no "thing" to see. That is the real emptiness." Hearing this, it's easy to form the thought, "This is emptiness! I see it!" This is not real emptiness, but a fabrication, a fake. This counterfeit emptiness, a mere idea, does not cut through the root of the three poisons. In the moment of seeing that mind essence is no "thing" whatsoever; we should not become entangled with any thought. Never speculate "Now it's empty!" or "This is not empty!" or "This is it!" or "This is not it!" In the very moment of looking, the real emptiness is instantly seen. But once you begin to think, "This is emptiness" it is artificial. The true emptiness, buddha nature, is naturally free from thought. So, when we start to think, "This is emptiness!" that is just a thought. We must discard the thought, "This is emptiness!"

This absence of all conceptual formulations is the special quality of the true Buddhist view. Other schools of spirituality may very well see the essence and understand that it's empty, yet they fail to let go of the idea of what emptiness is. Regardless of whether it is eternalism or nihilism, whatever formulation we concoct strays from the real nature itself. Self-existing wakefulness does not have to be thought of to be so.

Emptiness does not have to be made; it is self-existent. If you need to construct it, how can it be self-existing? "Self-existing" means it is not necessary to create it. Failing to acknowledge this is ignorance. The realization of natural emptiness is the only thing that can cut through thoughts. Thought cannot conquer thought. Moreover, when cutting through thoughts you simultaneously cut through the basis for the three realms of samsara. I expect you are all very intelligent; so pay careful attention to this. We all have something called self-existing wakefulness that we do not need to create or manufacture.

Nonconceptual wakefulness totally overcomes conceptual thinking. If nonconceptual wakefulness were merely another thought, it could not overcome thoughts. In the very moment of recognizing it, thoughts are cut through and overcome. Is there anything more wonderful than that?

As I said before, deliberate mindfulness is like pressing the switch to turn on the light of nonconceptual wakefulness. It is the preliminary, not the main part. To think that pressing the switch is the main part of practice is mistaken. Just as we cannot approach the main practice without undergoing the preliminaries, we cannot approach mind essence without deliberate mindfulness.

Often there is mention of several types of mindfulness: deliberate mindfulness, effortless mindfulness, dharmata mindfulness, wisdom mindfulness, all-pervasive mindfulness and so forth. These latter terms lay out in great detail the differences between the seven impure and the three pure bhumis. Of course, we could delve into this terminology intellectually, but that is not so beneficial at this time. The different stages have to be related to our personal experience.

The Dzogchen tradition describe six types of mindfulness. Other systems mention only two: deliberate and effortless. The first type is called mindfulness of deliberate attention. The second type is called innate mindfulness. The Dzogchen tradition phrases it this way: "Sustain primordially free awareness with innate mindfulness." There is no transformation involved here at all. It is the original state of awareness that is sustained by natural mindfulness. The ultimate is the "all-pervasive mindfulness" in which there is no distraction whatsoever. Awareness reaches as far as space reaches. It is unbroken and without interruption. Day and night, there is only all-encompassing awareness. All distraction has vanished into the state of dharmata. This is the dharmakaya of all buddhas.

Some people believe that they should just keep on meditating, and someday their egg will hatch and they will fly out of the shell and ascend to a completely different level. Actually, it's not like that at all. We should not think, "The awakened state must be something really special. If I practice this long enough, one day a door will open and I will see it and all the qualities will pour into me." It's pointless to have this kind of attitude.

If we really want something spectacular, we will indeed have opportunities for that, in what is called the "temporary meditation moods" of bliss, clarity and nonthought. These can occur, but such sensational experiences do not help to cut through thoughts. On the contrary, they generate even more fixation because we start to think, "Wow! What is that? This must be *it!*". Many subsequent thoughts arise in response to the fascination with these experiences.

As I mentioned before, realization involves a process called recognizing, training and attaining stability. It's similar to planting the seed of a flower. You plant it, water it and finally it grows up and blossoms. We are not like Garab Dorje, who, at the very instant of having mind nature pointed out, became a fully enlightened buddha without having undergone any training whatsoever. The moment of recognizing mind essence free from thought is like holding an authentic flower-seed in your hand and being certain of what it is. That itself is the self-existing wakefulness, the source of buddhahood. Enlightenment does not come from some other place.

TIREDNESS

COMPARED TO THE HABIT FROM COUNTLESS AEONS of being deluded, you have been training in the recognition of mind nature only a short time. It is impossible to attain stability in a few months or even a few years; it does not happen. It is necessary to be diligent, in the sense of persistence or constancy, totally effortless constancy. Think of how the string of a bow keeps the same tautness throughout its length: it is not that some spots are tightly drawn while others are slack; the string is evenly taut throughout. Likewise, the way to practice is not to sometimes push to recognize mind essence and then give up; it is a matter of being deeply relaxed from within and continuing in unfabricated naturalness. You have to become accustomed to this state, through the short moment of recognition repeated many times.

The stream of consciousness of an ordinary person is called the "continuous instant of delusion." That means every instant of time is wasted on deluded, dualistic involvement with some object. This is a strong habit, and it creates the circumstances for the next moment to follow in the same manner. Thus the third and the fourth moments ensue; and before you know it, months, years, lives and aeons have flown by. This continuous instant of delusion is a deeply ingrown inclination towards total diffusion in the confused state that has been going on and on for so long. This is not what we need to train in — we have already been doing so for countless lifetimes!

The opposite of this tendency is when we train in the "continuous instant of nonfabrication," which is rigpa, the awakened state itself. Through this unfabricated naturalness, without trying to do anything whatsoever, we counteract the ingrained habitual mode of the continuous instant of delusion, the creator of the samsaric state. The true yogi does not sustain involvement in discursive thought, fixation, or attachment. His mind is like space mingling with space. When there is no discursive thinking there is no delusion.

Nondual awareness in the case of a true yogi is that first instant of recognizing mind nature. Free of tangibility, it is the dharmakaya itself. Its essence is empty, its nature is cognizant and its capacity is unconfined, suffused with awareness. Regardless of whether we are talking about the confused or awakened state of mind, the present moment is always the unity of empty cognizance — there is no difference in this respect. But in the continuous instant of delusion, there is never any knowing of your nature — it is suffused with unknowing, with ignorance. In contrast, the continuous instant of nonfabrication is a knowing of your own nature. Therefore, it is called self-existing awareness — empty cognizance suffused with knowing.

When no discursive thinking, distraction or delusion occurs, this is the state of a buddha. We sentient beings distract and delude ourselves. We have forgotten our nature and fallen under the power of discursive thinking. Our minds are empty and cognizant but suffused with ignorance; we do not know. For a true yogi, the path of the buddhas is indivisible empty cognizance suffused with awareness. Once we have been introduced to our nature, become used to it and remain undistracted throughout day and night; we too are buddhas.

You should not become tired from alternately recognizing and forgetting mind nature. What is truly tiring is the state of deluded mind that creates completely pointless activity from one moment to another. It is a totally futile involvement that has been going on for untold lifetimes, but it is so habitual that we don't realize how exhausting it is. In the state of unfabricated naturalness, there is nothing to be tired of at all. It is totally free and open; it is not like doing prostrations or carrying a heavy load. How could unfabricated naturalness be tiring?

So on one side there is the exhaustion of the obscured "black diffusion" of mind, of habitual thought activity. On the other side is the good habit of trying to recognize rigpa each moment and not be distracted. What could be tiring is the effort of trying to recognize — "Now I recognize. Oops! Now I've forgotten! I became distracted and it slipped away." This kind of alertness may be a little too strenuous and deliberate. It can tire you out, whereas there is no way that recognizing and remaining in unfabricated naturalness can be tiring.

The antidote for exhaustion is, from the very beginning, to relax from deep within; to totally let be. Training in the awakened state of mind is not something you must keep up in a deliberate way. Rather, recognizing unfabricated naturalness is totally effortless. The best relaxation brings the best meditation. If you are relaxed from deep within, how can that be tiring? What is difficult is to be continually distracted; freely remaining in the totally unfabricated, undistracted nonmeditation, it's impossible for tiredness to occur.

Let me repeat again: what *is* exhausting is ordinary uninterrupted delusion, the mind thinking of this and that — the continuous spinning of the vicious wheel of anger, desire and dullness. We engage in such useless activity nonstop, both day and night. Once you have been introduced to the nature of mind, you could possibly tire yourself in your effort to be diligent. But if we are effortless, how can we be exhausted? We need to destroy the effort: that is what is making us tired. In the essence of awareness that is free from dualistic fixation, what is there to create? We need the best relaxation; the difficulty comes from not having this. If this relaxation does not come from deep within, definitely we will become tired. What becomes tired is the dualistic mind. Nondual awareness is like space — how can space become tired? The most excellent meditation is to be stable in nondual awareness.

In the beginning, when we start this training, the master will say, "Look into your mind! Look into your mind!" This watchfulness is necessary until you are used to it. Once that has happened you don't need to look here or there. You have caught the "scent" of the nature of mind. At that point, you do not need to struggle; the nature of mind is naturally awake. Remember, the naked state of awareness has been clouded over by the dualistic frame of mind, as expressed in thoughts of the past, present and future. When awareness is free of the thoughts of the three times, it is like being naked.

Unless we look into the nature of mind we will never recognize it. But this is true only in the beginning. Once you grow more familiar with it, there is no need to look here or there, or to do anything. Recognition happens spontaneously because of being used to recognizing, to some extent. When there is a subject and object in the recognition, this is none other than dualistic mind.

Machig Labdrön advised, "Tighten tight and loosen loose: there you find the crucial view." "Tighten tight" means simply to look into mind essence. Unless you look there is no recognition. "Loosen loose" means to totally let go of or disown any idea of recognizing. What is recognized here is that there is no "thing" to recognize. The awakened state is not a thing that can be identified or pinpointed. This is most essential. Without recognizing that there is no thing to recognize, you will always hold onto some idea about it. To hold on to the notion of recognition and a recognizer is conceptual. This thought is the root of samsara. It is not self-existing wakefulness; it is a fabrication. So first look and then loosen from deep within; then it is like space, wide awake. This is the samadhi of suchness, which is real and naturally stable. What is seen is free of substantiality. It is not a "thing."

Even though you have already recognized, if you start to formulate, "Now it's rigpa! I got it!" your mind essence becomes clouded over by thought. There is no need to confirm your experience by thinking, "Now I recognize *it!*" This is unnecessary; it's merely another thought that interrupts nondual awareness immediately. This dualistic frame of mind is what is tiring. The continuous noticing that takes place: "Hey, now it's there" or "Now it's not there!" This is exhausting, whereas the actual process of recognizing and being distracted from rigpa is not tiring at all, but happens quite spontaneously. That is called "nurturing the primordially free awareness with innate mindfulness." Innate mindfulness is unfabricated mindfulness. Right now we look into mind essence by means of contrived mindfulness. Nurturing the primordially free awareness with innate mindfulness means to be free of a conceptual frame of mind. Just remain in naturalness; whether it lasts or not is okay either way. When this moment of recognition is artificially extended, it turns into a dualistic state of mind.

It is not true for everyone that rigpa only lasts for a very short time. There are some people who through having practiced in the lives preceding this one possess the power of former training. For them, the moment of recognizing does last a little while. This is not impossible. It is not that everyone only experiences a mere glimpse of the awakened state before it vanishes.

To repeat an important point: what is recognized here is that there is no "thing" to recognize. Nondual awareness is not a *thing* that can be identified or pinpointed. This is most essential, because without recognizing that there is no thing to recognize, you will always hold onto some idea about the awakened state. Clinging to subject and object in the recognition is none other than a dualistic frame of mind. Recognize that there is no thing to recognize, and then totally let go. Remain without observer and observed. Someone may ignore this and instead think, "The meditation master told me there is self-existing awareness. I must see it! I must recognize it! I must keep it in mind!" These are all concepts. As long as there is something to identify or think about there is still concept. It is this dualistic mind of continually affirming or denying that is exhausting. Awakened mind is the primordially free naked state called dharmakaya. So, sustain that with natural mindfulness, without fabricating a subject and object. To have one thing looking at another only creates more thought.

As for the true view, it is incorrect to claim that there must be something that is recognized and that there has to be a recognizer. This duality is a subtle state of conceptual mind. As long as you do not cut the string of subtle concepts, there is no liberation from samsara because there is always something sustained and someone who sustains it. There may be no coarse subject and object fixation, but a very subtle fixation is still present. As long as there is a faint observer and observed, then the subject-object fixation has not yet been totally abandoned. As long as this is not abandoned, samsara is not left behind.

Do you know how a cat sometimes lies in ambush at a mouse hole? Some types of meditation are said to be like that. Whenever the mouse sticks its head out, the cat is waiting to pounce. He is waiting there tied up in hope and fear, hoping the mouse will appear and fearing that it will not. In the same way, in some meditation practices one sits and waits for the awakened state to take place. As soon as rigpa manifests, one immediately catches on to it: "I need to recognize rigpa! Aha! There it is, now I've got it!" Trying to catch the natural state is tiring!

It is much better to rest in a totally carefree state without attachment. Not attaching importance to anything is like an old person watching children play. Children talk, "Today I will be a minister, tomorrow I will be a king." The old person will not attach any reality to it. He will think whatever they do let them do it; it does not matter. In the same way, the old person that is nondual awareness completely lets go of attaching any importance to the arising and ceasing of thoughts. It is very exhausting if you have to keep track of the awakened state, thinking, "Now I recognize it. Now I'm distracted. Now I got it back again. Now I lost it!" This process is simply adding another thought to each moment. Just relax. Lean back and rest freely in the openness of basic space. Keeping track of every moment it is very tiring; anyone, no matter who, would become tired of doing that.

Tradition describes the three types of "freely resting" — as a mountain, as an ocean and as awareness. Let your body freely rest like a mountain. Let your breath freely rest like an ocean, meaning that your breathing is as totally unimpededly as an ocean when its surface is undisturbed. Let your mind freely rest in awareness; in other words, remain in the nature of mind. The awakened state is free of the thoughts of the three times. The present wakefulness is totally fresh; it does not arise, dwell or cease. So do not force that which is free of arising, dwelling or ceasing to arise, dwell and cease. Spend your life within these three types of freely resting.

In the moment of recognizing the authentic state of mind essence, the three poisons are interrupted, at least for a short while. When the three poisons are interrupted, the obscurations are purified; and when the obscurations are purified, rigpa is primordially free. This describes the inherent quality of awareness.

The example is used of switching a light on in a room that has been in pitch-black darkness for 10,000 years. The darkness disappears in the same instant that the light is switched on, doesn't it? The moment we recognize mind essence, the stream of deluded involvement in the three poisons is interrupted right there. It is purified. The moment of recognizing the awakened state simultaneously interrupts the obscurations and negative karma from the past, present and future. That is the incredibly great quality of the naked dharmakaya.

The present wakefulness free of the thoughts of the three times is the dharmakaya. There is nothing in this world more precious than dharmakaya. If our minds did not have this great capacity to recognize dharmakaya in a single moment, it would be quite pointless to train in it. A single instant of recognition can completely dispel the darkness of ignorance. Dharmakaya is not created by our meditation practice; it is already, primordially, present. All karma and obscurations are momentary and not inherent to the primordial dharmakaya. If you put a strand of hair into a flame, which remains? Only the flame; the hair is temporary. Similarly, dharmakaya is primordially present, while the thoughts of sentient beings are momentary. That is what is meant by both subject and object fixation being eradicated by recognition of mind essence. Dharmakaya in itself is free of subject and object.

Even though dharmakaya, buddha nature, is free of subject and object, the naked state can be momentarily veiled. Think of it like this: where you were born wearing clothes? No, you were born naked and you temporarily wear clothes. Take off the clothes, and aren't you naked again? This is the example for the naked dharmakaya, the basic state of all sentient beings.

This is the most profound state possible, and you should allow it to be by means of unfabricated naturalness. But sentient beings feel compelled to keep fabricating that which is unfabricated. We are constantly making or forming something in our minds. We contrive the natural state, first with the three poisons, that extends naturally to the 80 innate thought states, then all different kinds of aspects, such as the 84,000 types of disturbing emotions. That is the machinery that makes the whole of samsara spin. We are keeping awakened mind imprisoned: the naked state has been put in prison and is surrounded by 84,000 types of prison guards. Day and night it is encased in that prison cell; so now, rigpa needs to make its escape!

We have imprisoned the self-existing state in endless samsara, but all we need to do to break free is to recognize the primordially awake state. Right now our basic awareness is incarcerated in endless samsara. We think, "Now I'm doing this, next I'm going to do that. I'm seeing this; I'm thinking of that. I'm meditating on this. Now I'm forgetting, now I'm recognizing." We never leave it alone in unfabricated naturalness. All this is merely installing new bars in our prison. For example, thinking "I'm a Shravaka, I'm practicing Mahayana, now I'm doing Kriya Yoga, Anu Yoga, Dzogchen ..." — all these ideas about philosophical systems are simply imprisoning the awakened state. The more you let be, the more rigpa is allowed to surface.

When we truly actualize Ati Yoga it is like being released from prison. Becoming a shravaka or bodhisattva is like being served our parole papers. Practicing the three outer tantras is like we are about to be released. The prison door is almost open when we practice Maha and Anu. With Ati Yoga, it is as though someone has said, "Open the door. Walk out!" When you are fully realized, you are totally free; you are out! You are on your own. The prison guards of dualistic mind cannot kick you around or hold you any longer. You are free in nondual awareness. You are a free person; you are no longer in prison. If you want to stand straight, that's up to you; if you want to sit, you can do that too. In that moment of naked awareness, you are free; you are in charge.

The basic point is to train in this practice. When the sun of the naked state of dharmakaya rises above the highest peak of the three experiences of bliss, clarity and nonthought, it illuminates the whole world. Once you gain some stability in rigpa, then the involvement of dualistic mind is seen as really tiring. One thinks, "Why didn't I get tired before of all this thinking?" The awakened state is totally open and free, not holding anything. It is self-liberated and naturally free. There is no reason to be tired from it. What is really tiring are the three poisons, the five poisons, the 51 mental factors, the 80 innate thought states, and the 84,000 disturbing emotions; these are exhausting. When they cease, you will understand that all deluded karma is pointless, futile. We really have given ourselves a hard time. We have confined the open view; we have fixated and lost our freedom. We have been overtaken by endless thought activity, life after life after life, thinking one thought after another. There was never any stability in that. Deluded thinking is a charlatan, an impostor. Isn't it better to be totally open and carefree?

To keep score of the recognition and distraction that occurs in our practice is called "strenuous mindfulness"; it is not liberation. The awakened state itself is free from strenuous mindfulness. It is totally free, open, at ease, not difficult at all. Yet we have confined this open, free state in a narrow little space. How exhausting it is, to be under the oppression of dualistic mind!

THE TRUE FOUNDATION

Let me tell you another essential point: until you have truly taken to heart and assimilated their truth within your being, continue to train in the general and specific preliminaries. These are the reflections on the "four mind-changings" — the precious human body, on impermanence and mortality, on the consequences of karmic actions, and on the negative characteristics of samsaric existence. The specific preliminaries are: taking refuge and making prostrations, generating bodhichitta, Vajrasattva recitation, mandala-offerings, and guru yoga. It is common to all schools of Tibetan Buddhism to begin with these.

If we truly take the four mind-changings to heart, reflecting sincerely on the sufferings of the six classes of beings, we will not find it difficult to do these preliminary practices. Otherwise we might think it was okay to just lay back and have a good time eating and drinking, with an attitude like "Why bother to do exhausting things such as prostrations and mandala offerings?" In reality, these preliminary practices are the foundation for attaining complete enlightenment. When you sincerely understand that, you can see the reason for doing this "work."

However much you hear about the difficulties of obtaining a precious human body and the value of renunciation, the will to be free, such information will only benefit when you make these thoughts your own. Right now you have the freedom to do so. Make no mistake; these four reflections are the very basis for the path of enlightenment. To build a house you need a stable foundation; if the foundation is good then a hundred-storied tower can be built on top of it. If you want to become enlightened in this very body and life, you need to bring about a deep shift in attitude, a shift that can take place by reflecting on these four mind-changings. On the other hand, if you only want to enjoy life's pleasures, you'll find Dharma practice to be extremely tiring. You will lose interest in it eventually if you think these four thoughts are unimportant. In fact, you will not have any lasting interest in a spiritual path until you take them into your stream of being.

For example you hear talk about the view, about the teachings of Madhyamika, Mahamudra and Dzogchen. Through these, you can attain enlightenment in one body and one lifetime; such precious teachings do exist. But it is a mistake not to take the four mind-changings as your foundation. To rely only on teachings about the view is like trying to arrive somewhere that can only be reached by flying, when you only have the capacity for walking. If we do not have the proper foundation there is no way to progress.

Almost every Dharma system contains preliminary and main practices. The Buddha said, "Just as the steps of a staircase, you should also train step-by-step and endeavor in my profound teachings; without jumping over any step, proceed steadily to the end. Progress in Dharma is similar to the way a small child gradually develops its body and strength, from entering in the beginning up until the complete perfection." First are the teachings of the shravakas and pratyekabuddhas, and the levels continue like going up a staircase all the way up to the three profound views of Mahamudra, Madhyamika and Dzogchen.

It cannot be repeated too many times that you need a firm foundation. Unless you are someone of the highest capacity like Garab Dorje, it is not enough to have merely been introduced to the view without following that up with the preliminary practices. Needless to say, not everyone is of the highest capacity: the perfect conditions do not always manifest with a perfect teacher, a perfect student, and perfect teachings. Taking this into account, we have to examine ourselves honestly. We are ordinary people, and we are mistaken if we think otherwise. If from the start the four mind-changings have been a motivating force, then practicing the Dharma will not be difficult at all. Without embracing these we will only tire ourselves.

The very basis of our practice rests on taking these four mind-changings to heart.

Within the preliminary practices, all three yanas can be practiced in one session, on one seat. Taking refuge comprises the essentials of the Hinayana teachings; generating bodhichitta embodies the heart of the Mahayana teachings; and meditation and recitation of Vajrasattva comprise the very quintessence of the Vajrayana teachings. Thus, within a single session, we can cover all three vehicles and perform a complete Buddhist practice.

If we want to practice many extensive details, you can find hundreds of thousands of teachings in the Buddhist canonical collection. But it is impossible to practice them all in a single lifetime. Padmasambhava and other masters kindly extracted the essence of the teachings in developing the preliminary practices, which include all the instructions of the scholars and accomplished beings of India and Tibet. Every Vajrayana school contains these preliminary practices. Why? Because these are an excellent method for purifying obscurations and gathering the accumulations. Without purifying obscurations and gathering the accumulations we cannot reach the state of enlightenment. Compared to the main practice, the preliminary practices are considered more profound. If you want to grow a crop you need fertile ground: a hundred years of planting seeds on a stone will not yield a harvest. If these four thoughts, the four mind-changings, are not embedded in your stream of being, if you do not comprehend their depth, then you will not realize the true meaning. The highest teachings of Vajrayana have their base in the preliminary practices.

The four mind-changings are not beyond our comprehension. We are capable of understanding that having a human life is extremely rare and precious. Most people know that everything is impermanent, that with each passing day our life becomes shorter. If we have some degree of intelligence, we can trust that our actions have their karmic consequences. Finally, it's apparent that all samsaric states, being impermanent and unreliable, can never offer us lasting happiness. These are all things we can understand — but intellectual comprehension is not enough. We must take to heart and deeply assimilate this understanding within our stream of being.

All the great masters of the past practiced in this way. They gave up all worldly concerns and attached as much importance to mundane aims as we do to a gob of phlegm spat out onto the ground. No one ever thinks of picking up such an object, do they? We should try to cultivate that same detachment toward all samsaric states. The old Kadampa master said, "Give up your homeland; wander in unknown lands; be a child of the mountains; wear the mist as your garment; keep companionship with wild animals in jungles, forests, caves and mountain retreats." How were practitioners able to do this? Was it just by pushing themselves into enduring these hardships? No, they simply took to heart, clearly and genuinely, the four mind-changings. When we reflect on these four points and truly take them to heart, then practicing the Dharma in an authentic way is not difficult at all.

The measure of having taken to heart the preciousness of the human body with its freedoms and riches that are so difficult to find, is that we are unable to waste time. We are filled with deep joy at having attained something so precious and rare, and we want to put this treasure to full use. This sense of true appreciation, of rejoicing so deeply that one cannot sit idle, is the measure of having taken to heart the preciousness of the human body.

Another example for taking the four mind-changings to heart is that of a beautiful but vain maiden who notices that her hair has caught fire. She will not rest at ease for a single instant, but will immediately try to extinguish the flames. In the same way, if we have truly assimilated the four mind-changings, we will not hesitate for a single second, but will immediately try to practice the sacred Dharma.

People usually have the attitude, "Things do last; we live for quite some time." Of course, they know that there is impermanence, but they think that it does not pertain to the present; that it is something that "comes later on." For example, we might think, "This particular object will finally disintegrate; right now, however, it does exist and continues to do so. Things are therefore permanent." This attitude is contrary to how things really are.

134

Taking impermanence to heart means to acknowledge that nothing whatsoever lasts even from one moment to the next — especially our life. Our existence here in a physical body has no real permanence. We will die. We should develop this attitude, "I will die. I do not know when and I do not know how; but it is unavoidable!" Keep this feeling so acutely in your mind that you cannot bear to sit idle. Instead you will feel: "I have to do something truly worthwhile. I cannot let the time fly by. As each day and moment passes, I'm closer to death. Not only me — it's like this for everyone, but no one pays any attention." The measure of having taken to heart the thought of impermanence is a genuine understanding of our mortality and everyone else's. When you have this painfully acute understanding of the "suffering of being conditioned" and of the fact that time is continuously running out, you refuse to waste a single second on anything that is not Dharma practice.

As a further argument for impermanence, consider the universe in which we live. Usually people believe that the world is solid and real, but this is not true. It will not last forever, and in the meantime it is constantly changing with each passing moment. When the universe finally disintegrates, there will be an end to this world as we know it. It will be destroyed by the "seven suns," and the "one water" until the only thing remaining is space. Since space is uncompounded, it can never disintegrate; but everything within space vanishes — everything! Then a period of voidness will endure for a while until a new universe is formed. It in turn remains for a while — which is the time we are experiencing now — and again disintegrates and vanishes. These four major cycles — formation, abidance, destruction, and voidness — a world goes through constitute a great aeon and this process is repeated again and again. Nothing material is exempt from this endless process. By pondering this, our normal tendency to cling to permanence will naturally fall away.

Also consider the great noble beings who have appeared in this world. All the bodhisattvas of the past as well as all the buddhas who possessed incredible clairvoyance, wisdom and the capacity to transform an aeon into a second and a second into an aeon have passed away. The bodily forms of great noble beings are not permanent either. Please ponder this.

Consider the people who possessed great merit, power and dominion. Universal rulers, *chakravartins,* who wielded the "wheel of gold" controlled all four continents. Those possessing the "wheel of silver" reigned over three continents. Those possessing the "wheel of copper" governed two continents; and those possessing the "wheel of iron" still held command over one entire continent. They had the power to rule over all peoples. They could even dine with Indra on the summit of Mount Sumeru, seated on thrones of equal height, and then fly back into the human realm. But where are they now? They are all gone. Please realize that even people of great might also vanish.

Next, consider the many causes of death and the few circumstances for staying alive. There are 404 kinds of diseases, 80,000 kinds of attacks from evil spirits, and many other obstacles for life as well. All these surround us like gusts of wind in a great storm, while our life-force is like the flame of a candle or a butter lamp. There are very few reasons for this flame to remain without being extinguished. We usually believe that medicine prolongs life, but sometimes medicine administered in the wrong way can become the cause of death. Even the means of healing can cut life short. Please consider the many causes of death and the few circumstances that sustain life.

It is a small miracle that we wake up each morning. It is said that the difference between being alive or dead is a single breath. If you exhale and don't inhale, you are dead. That's all it takes. Nagarjuna said, "Since this is the case, it's amazing, a wonder, that one wakes up in the morning." It is not enough to merely hear or read about impermanence; you need to take it to heart.

In the cycle of teachings given by Padmasambhava called *Karling Shitro* — the *Peaceful and Wrathful Deities revealed by Karma Lingpa* — there is a very vivid image of the inevitability of our death. Imagine that you are standing on a half-inch-wide ledge on a sheer cliff overlooking an almost bottomless abyss, with a roaring river raging below. You cannot bear to look down. Only your toes can rest on the ledge, while your hands grasp two handfuls of grass the size of a goat's beard. You are hanging onto these two handfuls of scrub-grass that represent your life-span and life-force. At the same time, impermanence, in the form of two rats representing the Lord of Death and the Lord of Life, gnaw away the grass you are clinging to, piece by piece. Once the grass is consumed, there will be nothing left to hold onto. There is only one way to go: to plunge into the nearly bottomless abyss and the raging river. Your guardian spirits are present in the form of two crows who hover above you; but how can they help your desperate situation? So, you hang on while the rats eat up the grass, blade by blade. You have no chance of survival whatsoever.

This is our current situation. We as practitioners must vividly imagine Padmasambhava's teaching, which clearly points out our mortality and inescapable death. Please contemplate this well, because it represents how it truly is. Below is the "abyss" of the three lower realms. We do not have to think of anything other than that. Then ask yourself, "What can I do?" A true practitioner should take this to heart and meditate on it!

Our clinging to sense-pleasures, the desirable objects of the five senses, causes us to spin around in samsara. Here's another example from the *Karling Shitro* regarding attachment to sense-pleasures. Imagine you are sentenced to death and have been dragged before the executioner. Your head now lies on the chopping block and he raises the ax in the air above your neck. He's just about to strike when someone steps up to you and says, "I would like to present you with a beautiful consort, a magnificent palace, and countless luxuries and enjoyable experiences!" How will you feel, knowing the ax is about to fall? Is the prospect of enjoying all these sense-pleasures enticing in the least? This example from the *Karling Shitro* illustrates in a very vivid way the futility of our attachment to the five sense pleasures of samsara. Do we really think they will last? Practitioners, combine the metaphor with the meaning!

Trust in the consequences of your karmic deeds. All that takes place: the formation of the universe, its abiding, changing and disintegration, occurs without any creator or maker to initiate it. It is all the result of the karmic actions of sentient beings. This is an unfailing law.

Next, among the six classes of beings, all the different life-forms are basically painful. There is no place of permanent happiness within samsara, regardless of where you are reborn. As a hell being, you suffer from heat and cold; as a hungry ghost, you suffer from hunger and thirst, as an animal, you suffer from stupidity and being enslaved or eaten by others; while as a human being, a demigod or a god, you still suffer from various imperfections. If you reflect deeply upon these different samsaric states, you will find that none offers any sanctuary free from suffering and pain.

Longchen Rabjam meditated for many years in a place called Gang-ri Tökar, White Skull Snow Mountain, where he even lacked a proper cave. He took shelter for three years under a cliff overhang. His only possession, in terms of bedding and clothing, was a hemp-cloth sack. During the day he wore this as his garment, while at night it became his bedding. This single scrap of sackcloth also served as his seat during meditation sessions. At the entrance to this rock overhang grew a huge thorn bush. Whenever he had to go out and relieve himself, the thorns pierced his body in numerous places. While he was urinating outside, he would think, "It's really uncomfortable having to push past this thorn bush every day. I should hack it down!" Then, on his way back in, he would think, "On the other hand, maybe this is the last day of my life. Why should I spend it cutting down a bush? That's meaningless — I'd rather do something that has real significance, like train myself in the view, meditation and conduct. If this is my last day, I should spend it practicing. One never knows how much time one has left in life." So, he would forget about cutting down the bush and go back inside to continue his practice session. This went on day after day, and after three years he attained complete realization. And he never cut down the thorn bush. This is an example of how the reflection on impermanence can manifest itself in a great realized master like Longchenpa.

The whole point of the preliminary practices is to purify the negative karma and the obscurations we have created. This does not necessarily involve the pursuit of physical well-being. Doing prostrations and the other preliminary practices is not a matter of making ourselves as comfortable as possible. Trying to avoid pain is definitely not the style of an honest practitioner. It is the behavior of a Lhasa dignitary, who prostrates on top of a soft mattress with all kinds of cushioning devices on his knees, ribs, and elbows to ensure that the practice will not hurt in any way. This is called "VIP prostrations," and I assure you that this style does not purify any karma or obscurations whatsoever.

There is another way of prostrating, which is the style of Paltrül Rinpoche. You simply prostrate wherever you are; however the landscape may be. Whether you are prostrating in the main shrine-hall or outside atop rocks and grass, you bow down and stretch out, full of devotion, imagining that you are right in front of the objects of refuge. Paltrül Rinpoche always practiced outdoors in the vast meadows. He lived in a black yak-hair tent and he would often do prostrations outside while chanting the *Sukhavati Aspiration* by Karma Chagmey, a prayer to be reborn in the pure land of Buddha Amitabha. Because Paltrül Rinpoche never bothered with a prostration board or any cushioning devices, he eventually wore down through the grass and down into the soil, leaving a deep indentation in the ground the exact size of his body. This is how most Tibetan practitioners of the past prostrated. They did not dress up in special prostration gear and glide in an especially soft place so there would be no pain. Many people would draw blood from their hands. I have often seen people skin their foreheads and develop a callus, and sometimes skin their hands and knees. By performing 100,000 prostrations in this way you can definitely purify your negative karma and obscurations.

When we take a bath, we wash away the dirt and sweat that has accumulated on our skin. In fact, the whole reason for taking a bath is to clear away this accumulation. It's not that we leave half of it and say, "I took a bath so now I am clean," when we are still half dirty. In the same way, the point of the *ngöndro,* the preliminary practices, is to remove the obscurations and become pure. Therefore, the basic guideline for how to practice and how long to practice, is the extent to which we have purified our obscurations. There is no real guideline other than total purification!

The whole reason for doing prostrations is to completely purify misdeeds and obscurations, not to do easy, comfortable Dharma practice. That is not the aim in itself; neither is it self-mutilation. The point is to focus totally on the practice with proper motivation, with full devotion for the Three Jewels and compassion for beings, combined with diligence. This is the main thing. We should not be emerging from our bath or shower still dirty; remember this!

At the time of the Buddha, which was called the Age of Perfection, it was sufficient to do one complete set of 100,000 preliminaries in order to achieve complete purification. The next two ages that followed were called the "two-endowed" and the "three-endowed," meaning two and three repetitions were necessary. The fourth period, which we are in now, is called the "period of adhering only to the superficial attributes." At this time, it is not enough to do two times 100,000 or even three times 100,000 to achieve complete purification. In this age we must do four times 100,000, meaning four full sets of preliminaries.

Motivation, your attitude, is of primary importance when going through the preliminary practices. This attitude involves devotion for the Three Jewels and compassion for sentient beings, infused with diligence. If you train in the preliminaries with proper motivation they will turn out well: that is the first point. The second point is that negative karma and obscurations are embedded in the *alaya,* the all-ground. As long as this all-ground with its ignorant aspect is not purified, it will continue to form the basis for further obscurations and negative karma. So, what truly needs to be purified is the basic ignorance of the all-ground.

To achieve complete purification is the main point, not only when doing prostrations and taking refuge, but also during the other preliminary practices. After performing the visualization, try to remember the view of Mahamudra, Dzogchen or the Middle Way. At times, try to prostrate and chant while remaining in mind essence. This will increase the effect of the practice. It is said that when a practice is done correctly, with mindfulness rather than just doing it mechanically, the effect is multiplied 100 times. If the practice is carried out while in the state of samadhi, in other words while recognizing mind essence, its effect is multiplied 100,000 times. Since many people have great interest in recognizing the nature of mind, we need not set this aside while doing purification practices. On the contrary, we should unify the two aspects of practice: the accumulation of merit and the accumulation of wisdom.

By combining these practices with the recognition of mind nature, we combine the accumulation of conceptual merit with the accumulation of nonconceptual wisdom. By the accumulation of merit with a reference point, you manifest the two-fold rupakaya and purify the obscurations of disturbing emotions. By the accumulation of wisdom free from reference point, you realize the immaculate dharmakaya and purify the ignorant all-ground. The way to do this is, after bringing to mind and visualizing the objects of refuge, to look into who is performing this practice. If we can do a full prostration without losing the view of mind essence, that single prostration is equal to 100,000 prostrations. It's how we practice that makes all the difference.

For example, reciting the hundred-syllable mantra only once while resting undistractedly in mind essence has the same value as distractedly reciting the hundred-syllable mantra 100,000 times. So, how one carries out the practice makes an enormous difference. By looking into mind essence while prostrating, we are able to purify not just our obscurations and negative karma, but also the very ground of ignorance upon which all obscurations and negative karma are based.

Even though you may have already done a great deal of Buddhist practice over the years, if you want to attain realization, do not hold yourself back from doing as many of the preliminary practices as possible until you are totally purified. It is not the number that matter, but the degree of purification. The way to maximize this is by combining the accumulation of merit with the view. So keep the view you have been introduced to, whether it be the view of Mahamudra, the Middle Way or of Dzogchen, in mind when you are performing the preliminary practices. No matter which of the three great views you choose to practice according to the Tibetan tradition, each includes the preliminary practices.

A famous quote sums up the whole reason for these practices: "When obscurations are removed, realization occurs spontaneously." The only thing that prevents realization is our obscurations and negative karma; and the preliminary practices remove them. When the mind is totally stripped of obscurations, realization is like a wide-open, clear sky with nothing to obscure it in any way whatsoever. Habitual tendencies are like the smell of camphor — even when it is washed away, a faint odor lingers. It is the same with the obscurations that lie latently within the all-ground. Another famous quote says, "It is delusion to depend on any other method than these practices for removing obscurations, gathering the accumulations, and receiving the blessings of a realized master."

What is more valuable — a single diamond or a room full of glass beads? Similarly, our practice does not depend on quantity, on the number of repetitions we accumulate in order to get the practice over with. It is not at all relevant to make it known that we are one of those amazing individuals who have completed five or ten sets of preliminaries. Some people practice with distracted minds, rushing through the motions as quickly as possible as though it was a mechanical chore. Their sessions are carried out looking right and left, without paying any attention to what they are doing. What is necessary is to focus body, speech and mind one-pointedly on the practice — *that* is what purifies the negative karma and obscurations. This is the real thing, the authentic diamond as opposed to a mere roomful of glass beads.

My root guru, my uncle Samten Gyatso, did this himself. Throughout his entire life, he never missed a single day of doing 100 prostrations. He made the *ngöndro* part of his daily practice, even when he was old and very sick. He walked with the help of two canes, one in each hand, so that people used to say he walked on "four legs" like an animal. Yet, he still managed to do 100 prostrations each day. The *ngöndro* that he adhered to was the preliminary practices for *Chetsün Nyingtig*.

Samten Gyatso died when he was 64. I do not know what he practiced as a little boy. But from the time I met my uncle and from what others could remember about him, he never, until the day he died, spent a single day without going through the preliminaries. My father, Chimey Dorje, did the *ngöndro* practices for both *Chetsün Nyingtig* and *Künzang Tuktig* every day. Even though the *ngöndro* preliminaries are extremely simple, they are, at the same time, also extremely profound. I suggest that you do the preliminary practices every day; this will be both excellent and very beneficial!

To reiterate, once you have taken the four mind-changings to heart, you will have formed a solid foundation and Dharma practice will not be at all difficult. If not, it is like trying to build a house without a foundation. The great masters of the past, especially those in the Kagyü lineage, have said, "Because they are the foundation, the preliminaries are more profound than the main part." Lay the solid foundation that results not merely from having "done" the preliminaries by going through the motions, but from having taken to heart the four reflections and the four or five times 100,000 preliminaries. Then you cannot help practicing in a genuine way. But simply having repeated the mantras and having the idea, "Okay, I did it," will not be the foundation for higher practices.

Whoever truly takes to heart the preliminaries is said to act like a wounded deer who flees to a place of solitude, not just "acting" like a practitioner in the eyes of others. Milarepa said, "I fled to the mountains to practice in solitude because I was frightened of death. Through practicing, I realized the nature that is beyond birth and death. Now I have captured the stronghold of fearlessness." That is how to practice.

If we undertake these preliminary practices in an authentic way so that we feel we cannot afford to waste a single moment, we will be able to practice like Milarepa. This is a solid foundation. Whatever is built upon it, such as the main practice of yidam-deity, mantra and completion stage, Trekchö and Tögal, will be like the stories of a building that will remain firmly grounded and stable. It's not enough to strive for the higher teachings and ignore the real substance of the Dharma which is a change in attitude. Unless we can change our hearts at a deep and profound level, the samsaric traits of our personality will all remain, and we will still be seduced by appearances. As long as our mind is fickle, it is easy to become carried away in the chase of power and wealth or the pursuit of beautiful objects, in concerns of business and politics, in intrigues and deceit. It is easy to become an insensitive practitioner who cannot be "cured" or changed by the Dharma. Although one may have great theoretical understanding, it does not penetrate to the core. That state is like a butter skin that is not made flexible by the butter inside, even though it holds the butter.

So, do not grab at the higher teachings of Trekchö and Tögal. They are like the impressive wolf skin hats worn in Kham; they look very good, but what keeps your ears warm in the winter is the unimpressive collar of plain sheepskin! It's much more important to emphasize the preliminaries and lay a solid foundation: then whatever is built on top of that afterwards will make sense. Otherwise, it will be empty talk.

Most important of all, more crucial than the extraordinary practices of Trekchö and Tögal, are the general and the specific preliminaries. Without having taken to heart these mind-changings, whatever practice you do will never lead anywhere. Nothing can be built when there is no foundation to build on. You may already know this very well; it may not be the first time you are hearing this. My words may be like trying to give the reading transmission of OM MANI PADME HUNG to Avalokiteshvara. Nonetheless, I wanted to say this to refresh your memory.

STRAYING

IN MY TRADITION, TRUE SAMADHI is not an outcome of concentration, settling or focusing the mind. True samadhi is the original, empty and ungrounded state that is the nature of our awareness. This is not a product, not a thing that is kept or sustained through the act of meditating; not at all. It is a recognition of basic awareness that is allowed to continue.

We can have three kinds of thought activity. The first is called "surface thoughts." It is the normal coarse thinking whereby we label different objects in our field of experience and become involved in an emotional response towards them. The second type of thinking is an "undercurrent of thought." It is an ongoing mental commentary that we do not really notice. There is a third type of thought activity, a thought movement that we become involved in when we "meditate." We sit and keep subject and object: there is "me," or that which notices, and the state of "samadhi," this sense of clarity and awareness. This creates the feeling, "Now, this is the state and it is ongoing!" It is not fully formulated or obvious. Very often, meditation practice is an exercise in keeping up that conceptual state. Afterwards, we think that the meditation state lasted for quite a while. What really lasted was the subtle notion of subject and object, appearing as clarity, as a brightness, or as maintained mindfulness. This is not the state of true samadhi that is totally free of home-made constructs or fabrications. The key phrase here is "originally empty and ungrounded," a state that does not require our making at all.

People often experience a certain tiredness after this rather conceptual meditation. This fatigue is in exact proportion to how much effort was applied to maintain the state. Once given up, we notice how tired we are.

Try now in your meditation practice not to maintain anything whatsoever. We should be free not only from the superficial and underlying thoughts, but also from the deep-seated thought constructs as well, which are what conceptualize the meditation state.

The most important aspect of the view is to be free of holding any notions about it. Any idea we hold about the view is a chain. No matter what kind of chain a bird is anchored by, it cannot fly. Any concept held during the meditation state is like a shackle.

Especially be free from the subtle notions of "sustainer and that which is sustained." That which is sustained is what we hear or read about: some kind of awareness, a wide-awake state. The sustainer is the judge who judges whether it is happening or not. If it does not occur, then we try to restore it, which is the act of sustaining. True meditation training should be free from sustainer and sustained.

The ultimate view is the same, regardless of whether we call it Dzogchen, Mahamudra, or Madhyamaka. It is often called "cutting through" or the "thorough cut." Like this string in my hand [Rinpoche holds up a protection cord], the string of thought formation is what keeps samsara continuing. Among the five aggregates, this is the aggregate of formation that is constantly perpetuated by our thinking. It is one of the three kinds of thought mentioned above. When we sit down to meditate, we clear away the normal coarse conceptualizing. By being mindful, we are not really overcome by the undercurrent of unnoticed thoughts. Yet, what happens then is that we are left with, "Now it's here, I am not distracted." Or "This is it, oh yes, right," which goes on and on throughout the session. We are not aware that we are formulating something and continuously keeping it in mind. How exhausting!

To think, "This is the empty state" is the subtle thought movement that occurs during meditation. When resting in the true view we do not need to formulate anything whatsoever. The nature of mind is, already, originally empty and ungrounded. Simply recognizing this and letting it be is the view. The best relaxation yields the best meditation. Relaxing should occur not just from the outside, but from deep within — totally letting be. That is different from keeping one-pointed in body, breath and mind.

In Dzogchen practice, as I have mentioned, one of the key points is "short moments, repeated many times." With short moments we do not become too tired during practice. Not practicing short moments, many times; but trying to sustain a continuous state is a form of attachment. It is not the same as mundane attachment that we leave behind during our meditation. Instead there is attachment to the "taste" of the view, the feel of it. We fear it will slip through our fingers, fall apart, or disappear because of our distraction. To counteract that, we hold the notion of the view and try to maintain the state continuously. That is still attachment and attachment is what makes samsara survive.

I am not directing any blame toward you. This is merely how samsara is. It is a perpetuation of the five aggregates. We need to be free of all five aggregates by means of genuine meditation training. Therefore, it does not help to sit while continuing the aggregate of formation.

The five aggregates are very subtle — the act of cognition, the act of forming conceptual states, the act of perception and so forth. The five aggregates are sustained in the most subtle way by the momentary forming of thoughts. Unless you can step out of that, you cannot step out of creating further samsara. This is an essential point.

The most important is to be free from the fascination, the subtle clinging to the feeling of meditation. First we totally relax. We get so relaxed and enjoy such a smooth, free feeling that sometimes we do not notice our physical body anymore. We experience, "This is so much nicer than the normal state. I like it! I should feel like this all the time! I don't want to lose it. I'll see if I can just keep it going." This frame of mind is nothing other than attachment. Isn't it attachment we should try to step out of? The best way to do that is to practice short moments repeated many times.

The subtle attachment, the "re-forming" of samsara with each passing moment, may seem very safe because it is a so-called meditation state. Nevertheless, attachment is, no matter how subtle, our arch enemy, the old demon who returns to stir up the samsaric storms of disturbing emotions.

All beings have buddha nature. What exactly is this buddha nature? It is original wakefulness. Physical space is empty. Our nature is also empty but it is different from physical space, because of the knowing quality. If our nature were merely like physical space, there would be neither wakefulness nor dualistic consciousness. But we have both. Although we possess the buddha nature of original, nondual wakefulness, it seems to be overcome or occupied by our dualistic frame of mind that always experiences in terms of subject and object. Even during meditation, there is the sustainer and that which is sustained. This is quite different from the buddhas. That which prevents buddha nature from remaining stable in itself is the tendency toward dualistic consciousness. "Buddha" simply means that dualistic consciousness is not overtaking the buddha nature, itself. The buddha nature is stable, without any duality.

When someone has a court case, they argue about what is true and what is false. Court cases are usually about two opposing standpoints or claims. During the court session, the argument takes place and finally the case of which is true and which is false is settled. Arriving at the view is like that. The samsaric state is on one side in the courtroom and the enlightened state is on the other side. We have to settle which is and which is not true. The final verdict is that dualistic consciousness is at fault while original wakefulness is faultless and wins the case.

The training in true samadhi begins after we have settled the court case; then, you can train in what is true. To arrive at what is true, we simply have to look very carefully. Afterwards we can indeed settle the case about how the nature of our mind is. If we try to find it, we cannot. The nature of mind can never be found as a "thing," as a lump waiting somewhere to be unearthed. Even if we continue searching for a billion years for that "thing" called nature of mind, we can never find it in a concrete, material form. Why, because it is empty. We can settle this through our experience when we look for the mind. We can personally discover this and finally say, "Yes, it is empty, I have looked for it and I cannot find it."

Yet, at the same time, it is not a complete blank or void, such as nothing whatsoever because we can still feel, know and experience. That is totally obvious, right? We can settle that case as well. Now there should be no doubt, no suspicion that the nature of our mind is empty and cognizant. Make sure you settle this once and for all.

The word "settled" or "decided" in Tibetan literally means "touching the horns." When two yaks are involved in a head-on collision, their horns will glide and touch base. One lone yak cannot do that. It takes two. You must have two things — one that is false and one that is true. When you touch base, it becomes obvious which is which.

When the Buddha says, "The nature of mind is empty," it is not enough to simply hear that. We need to discover it by ourselves. When we look for the nature of mind and do not find it, at that point we collide head-on with the truth. The mind is not just empty but also cognizant. While perceiving, it is still empty. Is this something we need to do — make the mind empty? Is it our making or not? No, it is already empty. This is what is called "originally empty and ungrounded." All we must do is acknowledge that this is how it already is. Apart from that, meditation is not something we need to sit and do to make mind primordially empty and ungrounded. We simply need to allow it to be what it already is. That itself is the training. Acknowledging this does not tire you out.

This is why it is so important to recognize the view. At the point of genuinely recognizing the view; there is only a single sphere, the single identity of the three kayas. The moment we recognize, nirvana is no longer something to be achieved and samsara is no longer something to be abandoned. This is how samsara and nirvana "flow together" and are contained within a single sphere. In general terms, samsara is definitely to be abandoned and nirvana is to be attained. In all practicality how are we going to get rid of samsara and attain nirvana? This is where the important quote comes in, "Knowing one thing, liberates everything."

When we go beyond accepting and rejecting, everything is unified. As long as we accept and reject, there is still some attachment and clinging. Tibetans sometimes say of a meditator, "Awesome! That yogi is really beyond fixation. He doesn't accept or reject anything. Now his fixation collapsed. He's like the sky." If we think we need to get rid of the thinking and attain wisdom; there are still two thoughts; the thought of abandoning one thing and achieving something else. This is accepting and rejecting. We still nurture this duality — one thing to eliminate, another to be gained. Accepting and rejecting is still subtle thinking. Once we let go of fixation, there is no accepting and rejecting.

In a previous chapter I quoted Vimalamitra mentioning three types of liberation. One is when a thought is freed like meeting a person you already know. The second is like a knot on a snake being untied by itself. The third is like a thief entering an empty house. This is talking about degrees of stability in the natural state. Otherwise the practice becomes as the saying: "knowing how to meditate but not how to be free, isn't that like the meditation gods?" Meditation gods are beings stuck high up in the highest levels of samsara called the "summit of existence." They are meditating, but do not be like them.

In Bangkok there are some unfortunate examples of meditation gods who supposedly are called arhats. The bodies of a few monks are preserved in a state in which they are neither dead nor alive; the perfect example of knowing how to meditate but not how to be free. It's been quite a few years since they "passed away" and have remained in a blocked state. They are in a "frozen emptiness," in a state of cessation that is not allowed to dissolve. This state of cessation happens before really passing away.

When I was in Malaysia, a monk came back from Bangkok and said "My teacher is still there in his body. He looks exactly the same. He is not rotten. He has not decomposed. I didn't dare to cremate, so I returned." These people are in meditation not liberation. This is what it comes down to when saying you do not gain enlightenment through shamatha. Shamatha always has a reference point. These beings are immobilized in that reference point which does not break up once you have become practiced in it. It is of course a quite impressive state of meditative concentration; but, to stay in one stable thought cannot be called liberation.

Remaining in that state after we have seemingly passed away means that our life span, merit and power have been all used up but still we stick around. If you burn the body you make the bad karma of killing it. It is very difficult to revive such a person; you need a yogi, a real meditator for that. The best is to perform the transference of consciousness for him. The state of cessation has a time limit and at some point the person wakes up again. Then he thinks "Oh no! I've been wasting all this time. It was totally pointless. It was no use at all!" He develops wrong views, regret, and anger; and such bitterness can easily "open the door" to a rebirth in hell. "I have used all these years meditating and I have not gotten even a cup of water's worth of benefit!" The duration of this state, dependent on the force and stability behind it, can last for many years.

There were many meditators like that in the eastern part of Tibet. Some Chinese working in the area went into the caves where the bodies trapped in inert shamatha were sitting. They cut open the stomachs and took out a substance that is used to make gun powder. Some of the body's insides were almost like red fresh meat. The heart, the intestines everything was there. I have heard that in some caves there were five or six of them sitting together. They can remain for a thousand years. They sit, not looking; their eyes are not open. The body remains unmoving, like in hibernation. The state of mind is kind of stupidity, though. I have not gone there myself, but another tulku in Kham went and told me there are three or four of these dried-up meditators sitting there. He did not know for how long. These Chinese workers cut up many and wrecked them.

In the Tantras there is a certain technique called the "method to revive a rishi." You have to soak the body in lukewarm water for a long time. The body will then start to move a little; the energies start to circulate. You pour medicine in the belly. You give mouth to mouth resuscitation. Slowly they will begin to breathe again. The master who does this, whispers in the ear "Now wake up from the state of cessation. You have been on an errant path." I have not seen the text but it does exist.

That kind of text is at the same time a pointing out instruction for vipashyana. What they say is "All right, you have done very well. Now it is enough shamatha. Now you should practice the essence of this state of shamatha, which is called vipashyana." I do not know exactly how long, but this frozen state has its own measure or length. When the force is used up or when the virtue is exhausted, because it is virtue in a way, naturally the person revives, wakes up again. Just like waking up from a dream. Finally when they wake up, they pass away very soon after.

There is another similar story involving my father Chimey Dorje. One time he went for a longevity ceremony to a house in which the cook was possibly a very diligent shamatha meditator. Before in Eastern Tibet they served tea from large clay tea pots. During the ceremony he walked in through the doorway holding such a tea pot. He was just standing there, without going in or out. He became stuck in a state of inert shamatha. My father said "Do not disturb him or wake him up. Otherwise he will drop the kettle and it will break all over the place." Such tea kettles are very hot. So Chimey Dorje allowed him to stand there holding this big pot of tea. He said "Let's see how long it lasts. Let him be." It took three or four hours and nothing happened. People began to get afraid he would not wake up or he would drop the whole thing. Chimey Dorje got off his seat and walked over to him. Close to his ear he whispered his name. He woke up. Then my father asked him what happened. The cook answered back, "What do you mean what happened? I am walking in with the tea." He was very diligent so he must have made good progress in some kind of inert shamatha state.

Here is another story about going astray in shamatha. A lama from the Eastern Tibetan province of Golok came to see the great Jamgön Kongtrül Lodrö Thaye. The lama told Jamgön Rinpoche that he had stayed in a retreat hut meditating for nine or ten years, "My practice is quite good now. At times I have some degree of clairvoyance. Whenever I place my attention on something, it remains unshakable; I feel so quiet and serene! I experience a state totally without thoughts and concepts. During long stretches of time I experience nothing but bliss, clarity and nonthought. I would say that my meditation has been rather successful!"

"Oh what a pity!" was Jamgön Kongtrül's response.

The meditator left slightly downcast, only to return the next morning. "Honestly, Rinpoche, my practice of samadhi is good. I have managed to equalize all mental states of pleasure and pain. The three poisons of anger, desire and dullness have no real hold over me anymore. After meditating for nine years, I would think that this level is quite good."

"Oh what a pity!" retorted Jamgön Kongtrül.

The meditator thought, "He is reputed to be an eminent master beyond jealousy, but it sounds to me as if he is slightly jealous of me. I wonder!"

He then said, "I came here to ask you about the nature of mind because of your great reputation. My meditation during time day is fine; I'm not asking about that at all. I'm quite satisfied! What I want to ask about is how to practice during the night; that is when I experience some difficulty."

Jamgön Kongtrül's reply was again just "Oh what a pity!"

The lama thought, "He really is envious of me! He probably doesn't have a fraction of the clairvoyant powers I do!"

When the meditator explained his clairvoyance, "For me it is no problem at all to see three to four days into the future," Jamgön Kongtrül again said, "Oh what a pity!"

The meditator left for his quarters. He must have begun to doubt himself, because after some days he returned and said, "I'm going back to my retreat. What should I do now?"

Jamgön Rinpoche told him, "Don't meditate any more! From today on, give up meditating! If you want to follow my advice, then go home and stay in retreat for three years, but without meditating even the slightest! Do not cultivate the state of stillness even in the slightest!"

The meditator thought to himself, "What is he saying! I wonder why; what does it mean? On the other hand, he is supposedly a great master. I will try it out and see what happens." So he said, "All right, Rinpoche," and left.

When back in retreat, he had quite a hard time trying not to meditate. Every time he simply let be, without the attempt to meditate, he always found himself meditating again. Later he said, "That first year was so difficult! The second year was somewhat better." At this point, he found that in the "act of meditating" he had simply been keeping his mind busy. Now he understood what Jamgön Kongtrül meant by saying "Do not meditate."

The third year he reached true nonmeditation, leaving deliberate cultivation totally behind. He discovered a state utterly free from doing and meditating; by simply leaving awareness exactly as it naturally is. At that point nothing spectacular took place in his practice, no special clairvoyance either. Moreover, his meditation experiences of bliss, clarity and nonthought had vanished, after which he thought, "Now my meditation practice is totally lost! I better go back and get more advice!"

Returning before Jamgön Kongtrül and relating his experience, Rinpoche replied, "Right on! Right on! Those three years made your meditation successful! Right on!" Jamgön Kongtrül continued, "You don't need to meditate by deliberately keeping something in mind, but also don't be distracted!"

The meditator said, "It may be due to my former training in stillness, but, actually, the stretches of distraction are quite short. There isn't much distraction anymore. I feel I have discovered what you meant. I experience a state which is not created through meditation yet which lasts for a while, by itself."

"Right on!" Jamgön Kongtrül said, "Now spend the rest of your life training in that!"

That was the story of a meditator from Golok who was later known to have reached a quite high level of realization.

UNITY

DEVELOPMENT STAGE AND COMPLETION STAGE, two main aspects of Vajrayana practice, are essentially two aspects of mind essence: emptiness and cognizance. Ultimately, these two aspects are an indivisible unity. To further understand this, consider how the four empowerments are conferred at the beginning of the Vajrayana path. The first empowerment, the vase empowerment, introduces the indivisible unity of appearance and emptiness. The second empowerment introduces the unity of clarity and emptiness, or luminosity and emptiness. The third empowerment introduces the unity of bliss and emptiness. Finally, the fourth empowerment introduces the unity of awareness and emptiness. The specific intent of each of these four empowerments is different, but the essential principle of all four is one: to introduce the indivisible unity of emptiness and cognizance.

This unity of these two is exactly what is meant by the unity of development and completion. The stages of development and completion are at the same time the very methods used to realize this essential principle. To attain stability in the manifest, cognizant aspect we need the development stage. To attain stability in the empty aspect, we need the completion stage, samadhi. The ultimate fruition of these two stages is the "kayas and wisdoms," which constitute the true buddha nature. When our ordinary body and the mind are refined they are the kayas and wisdoms, the former supporting the latter.

To meditate on a deity, we need to train in the *kaya*-aspect, the manifest aspect that we visualize. The identity of the kayas and wisdoms is emptiness. Although everything is said to be empty, the awakened state is not empty of kayas and wisdoms. Kaya and wisdom are also called body and wakefulness. In the awakened state, this body is an unconstructed "body of space," the unconstructed dharmakaya. The awakened mind is dharmadhatu wisdom. So, in the case of a buddha, on the dharmakaya level, body is dharmakaya, the body of wisdom qualities, while wakefulness is the dharmadhatu wisdom, an all-encompassing wakefulness. On the sambhogakaya level, body is a form of rainbow light, while wakefulness is the manifestations of its five wisdoms. On the nirmanakaya level, body is called the nirmanakaya, which means the body of magical apparition, comprised of the "vajra body with the six elements" of earth, water, fire, wind, space, and consciousness. The wakefulness aspect is the knowledge that sees the nature of things as it is and the knowledge of perceiving all existent things. At the most basic level, to find the real source of the kayas and wisdoms we need to realize both development and completion stages. On a more subtle level the deities will appear spontaneously in the bardo. The most subtle level is to gain stability in the practices of Trekchö and Tögal. Tögal is the manifest aspect, in which the bodies of the deities actually arise, while Trekchö is the empty aspect.

There are two expressions used in this context: abiding in the ground and manifesting from the ground. Abiding in the ground means that the kayas and wisdoms, the unity of manifest and empty, are from the beginning the basic component of buddha nature. One way to facilitate the manifestation of the deities is through visualizing them or reciting their mantras. By applying the methods of the development stage, we activate or manifest these qualities present within the ground. This is called "manifesting the ground," and it is what the development stage is all about.

The development stage is not a real meeting with the actual deity but a facsimile, a likeness. We cultivate this likeness, because our minds have fallen under the power of habitual tendencies, delusions, various thought patterns and negative emotions. To remedy this, we engage in "white training" — we think about celestial palaces, pure deities, and so on. We are not emptying ourselves of impure thoughts, but we can temporarily stop them. Due to the kindness of the buddhas, we can purify an immense amount of bad karma by practicing development stage. Really, we have to acknowledge the tremendous importance of the development stage.

When training in the development stage we attempt to manifest a semblance of enlightened qualities. These are not yet the real, authentic qualities; they are just a semblance. Think of how, during a lama dance, an ordinary monk will don a mask and dance around in an elaborate costume pretending to be an actual deity. The development stage is a similarly make-believe practice. Nevertheless, by imitating our intrinsic qualities we purify our habitual tendencies to perceive and fixate upon an ordinary solid reality. These obscurations are purified because the development stage engenders a simulation of our true, innate qualities.

Take the example of our habitual idea of living in a solid house. To combat this, we try to grow used to the idea that our environment, our dwelling place, is a celestial palace made of rainbow light. Instead of perceiving our ordinary body, we try to perceive our body as the pure, insubstantial form of a deity. Instead of ordinary conversations, we try to perceive all communication as the praise of enlightened qualities. Instead of fixating on sense impressions, we present them as offerings to the awakened ones. All these activities are not mere superficial ways of spending our time: they are profound methods of purifying the habitual tendencies that obscure our buddha nature. We should never believe that the development stage is useless, because it is most definitely not. Rather, to engage in the practice of the development stage creates immense merit. The true development stage is known as "instantaneous recollection." This means the deity is already present in the mandala of our mind, so we do not need to make it present with our hands or intellect. We merely need to think that we are Buddha Samantabhadra, for instance, and that's enough.

The way of starting the development stage is extremely profound. There are four ways in which sentient beings take rebirth in form: by means of an egg, a womb, heat-and-moisture, or instantaneously. Correspondingly, there are four ways of appearing as the deity that counteract the habitual tendencies of these four types of rebirth. The densest type is the "twice-born" or egg type of rebirth, whereby one is first born in an egg and then later emerges from the egg. The fastest and highest of the four types of rebirth is the instantaneous type. This is purified by the instantaneous recollection of the deity, whereby in a single instant we imagine that we are already in the full-fledged form of the deity.

As sentient beings, we have a body and a dualistic frame of mind. The source or root of these is identical with the source of the awakened state, with its manifold qualities and characteristics. Everything appears from the essence that we call buddha nature. Enlightened Body is the unchanging quality within buddha nature, enlightened Speech is the unceasing quality, and enlightened Mind is the unmistaken, undeluded, and unbewildered quality. In this way, enlightened Body, Speech and Mind are already present within our stream-of-being. How they manifest depends upon whether we are a sentient being or a fully awakened one.

There is no way to separate appearance and emptiness. We cannot throw one away and embrace the other. The final state of fruition, the "unified state of Vajradhara," is nothing other than the unity of emptiness and cognizance, or the unity of kayas and wisdoms. Ponder this: within Dzogchen, Trekchö and Tögal are a unity. Kayas and wisdom are a unity. Development and completion stage are a unity. All these are indivisible. Ultimately, appearances and emptiness, or cognizance and emptiness, are an indivisible unity.

There's a saying among the masters of the past: "When some swear to development, and some to completion, development and completion will then pick a fight." This saying is true. If we look closely at people's attitudes, we will find that some people say, "The development stage is really meaningful because there's something to do and to achieve. One can think of different things, get involved, apply methods, undergo some kind of transformation and reach fruition. Actually *doing* some kind of practice has significance, but the completion stage leaves us with nothing to do. It's just primordially empty; it seems quite meaningless to spend time on that." Other people say, "Sitting and imagining this and that during the development stage is all fake; one is only fooling oneself by making up superfluous scenarios. The original, natural, spontaneously present state of the completion stage is the real thing."

Both of these statements display a lack of understanding of how our basic state really is. Development and completion are already a unity. To know that is to know what *is* to be true. What prevents us from acknowledging the original state, which is the indivisible unity of experience and emptiness, of cognizance and emptiness, is nothing other than our own conceptual way of thinking. Our conceptual thinking splits a unity into a duality where no duality really exists. We form concepts based on a home-made division of subject and object, appearance and emptiness.

The only way to truly heal that constantly re-occurring split is by training in the practice in which there is no split and never was — the natural unity of development and completion. There is only one way to do that: through being introduced to and becoming stable in the state of samadhi in which emptiness and cognizance has never been divided in any way whatsoever. This state is an intrinsic unity; it is not that something somehow *becomes* unified.

To repeat, the principle to be understood here is that the qualities of awakened Body, Speech and Mind are already present within buddha nature. This buddha nature is called by many names, such as *rangjung yeshe*, meaning self-existing wakefulness, or awakened mind. Whatever the name, these enlightened qualities are already present. "Body," in this context, means the unchanging or abiding essence. "Speech" means the unceasing luminous presence of wakefulness. "Mind," in this context, means the undeluded, awakened capacity that radiates in an all-encompassing way as wisdom, loving compassion, the ability to save others, buddha activity, and so forth. In short, it is not necessary to unify emptiness with cognizance, but rather to realize the original indivisibility of these two aspects.

When practicing the development stage, we call upon the buddhas to approach from the pure realm of Akanishtha and dissolve into us. This is an incredibly profound method of dealing with the unwholesome dualistic mental patterns we have of separateness. They are purified because the practices involved in the development stage are their very opposites.

Our buddha nature that we already possess is like a basic capital to be invested. According to my tradition there are three levels of inner Vajrayana practice: Mahayoga, Anu Yoga and Ati Yoga. Mahayoga is embodied within Anu Yoga and Anu Yoga within Ati Yoga. All three of these yogas should be embodied within the sadhana practice, while the sadhana practice is embodied within personal application. In this way, everything comes down to our personal application. The special quality of Vajrayana, that which makes this vehicle superior, is described by this famous statement: "Although the aim is identical, there is no delusion," meaning there is complete understanding of the profound methods.

For a person on the path, there are two ways to unify development and completion. First, you practice the development stage, for instance by thinking, "I am Padmasambhava; I'm wearing a crown on my head and such-and-such garments, and I'm holding these various attributes in my hands." After that, you look into, "Who is it that imagines all this?" At that moment, it is seen that that which imagines or visualizes all this is empty, and at the same time cognizant. This empty knowing is called completion stage. This method is called "following the development stage with the completion stage."

The other approach is to let the development stage unfold from within the completion stage. Here you start out by looking into mind essence, allowing the awakened state of mind to be an actuality. Without leaving this state of nondual awareness, you then allow the visualization to take place. The very expression of nondual awareness then takes the form of a celestial palace, the form of Padmasambhava and all the other details of the mandala. The nondual state of awareness is unimpeded, just like images being unimpededly reflected in a mirror.

While unwholesome or egotistical thought-forms cannot arise as the expression of the awakened state, pure forms, such as the celestial palace, deities and so forth, can occur without leaving the state of rigpa. This is because the duration of recognizing rigpa resembles a clear mirror that unobstructedly reflects everything. If there is no recognition of our nature involved, we are like a stone that lacks the reflecting power of a mirror.

The unity of the development and completion stages means that the forms of the deity, palace and so forth are all manifest, meaning visible, in your experience while at the same time nondual awareness remains undistracted. There is no real division between manifestation and awareness. Understand that the unity of the development and completion stages is, in essence, the unity of experience and emptiness.

Karmapa Mikyö Dorje, the great Vajradhara of the Kagyü lineage, is the chief figure in the famous *Guru Yoga in Four Sessions*. One of its supplications says: "Visible, yet empty; empty, yet visible. The indivisible unity of being visible and empty is the form of the guru. I supplicate the guru's form." There is another verse for Speech and a third for Mind. What does this mean? It means that there *is* perception occurring, something is perceived, although, at the same time, that which perceives is empty. This indivisible nature of perceiving while being empty is, itself, the form of the guru. This is the ultimate enlightened Body and realizing this is the unity of development and completion.

It is the same with Speech or sound — it is "Audible yet empty, empty yet audible. The indivisible unity of being audible and empty is the Speech of the guru. I supplicate the guru's Speech." This covers not only so-called "external" sound, but, also an intrinsic sound called the spontaneous sound of dharmata that is mentioned in the Dzogchen teachings. This intrinsic sound is empty; that which hears the sound is empty as well. The indivisible unity of sound and emptiness is the Speech of the guru.

The third verse says: "Blissful yet empty; empty yet blissful. The indivisible unity of bliss and emptiness is the Mind of the guru. I supplicate the guru's Mind." Bliss, in this context, does not refer to the conditioned bliss that has a beginning and an end. It means the intrinsic absence of pain. When painful conceptual thought activity is absent, that is called "bliss." This basic state is empty. This emptiness, which is at the same time blissful, is the Mind of the guru. "I supplicate the guru's Mind of bliss and emptiness."

In the Nyingma lineage, as well, there is a pointing-out of the ultimate practice of deity, mantra and samadhi that links appearance and emptiness, sound and emptiness, and thought and emptiness. This is mentioned in the renowned *Supplication in Seven Chapters* to Padmasambhava. The first verse begins with: "Whatever occurs in your field of vision…" This means whatever you see, whether it is beautiful or ugly. "…do not accept or reject. Just rest in the state wherein appearance and emptiness are indivisible. This is the Form of the guru. I supplicate the form of Padmakara."

The next verse is about sound: "Whatever you hear, whether harsh or pleasant, do not accept or reject, but rest naturally in the unity of sound and emptiness. Indivisible sound and emptiness is the Voice of the guru. I supplicate the Voice of Padmakara."

The third is about thoughts: "Whatever occurs in the realm of the mind, no matter which of the three or five poisons arise, do neither welcome nor escort them. Let them naturally dissolve in the state of awareness. This naturally liberated mind is the Mind of the guru. I supplicate the Mind of Padmakara."

We begin training in the unity of development and completion with the three samadhis. The samadhi of suchness is a state that is awake, utterly open and unimpeded. This is the state within which the visualization of the deity can really occur. Nothing is blocked: this visualization can freely take place because awareness is not blocked. Neither are we unconscious. This is why the samadhi of illumination can freely take place out of the samadhi of suchness. From the samadhi of illumination, the samadhi of the seed-syllable can freely take place. If this were not the case, why would the buddhas teach it?

Yet, once the continuity of nondual awareness is broken and lost; the dualistic expression occurs as conceptual thinking. Conversely, since nondual awareness is unobstructed, its expression is of course also unobstructed, and can take any form whatsoever, such as the body of Padmasambhava with all its garments and attributes. Once the samadhi of suchness slips away, then this unobstructed display of nondual awareness is no longer possible. That's why every instruction in development stage mentions beginning with the three samadhis.

Among the three samadhis, the samadhi of suchness corresponds to dharmakaya and emptiness. The samadhi of illumination corresponds to sambhogakaya and cognizance. The samadhi of the seed-syllable, which is the unity of emptiness and cognizance in the form of a seed-syllable that becomes the deity, corresponds to nirmanakaya.

The external example is that dharmakaya is like open space, while sambhogakaya is like sunlight. Sunlight unfolds within space. The sun need not go somewhere else to shine. When there is space and sunlight, the rainbow that is nirmanakaya can appear. Please understand how this metaphor illustrates the three samadhis.

Again, what is the unity of the completion stage and the development stage? During the completion stage there is simply the recognition of mind essence itself. At the same time, its expression unfolds as the development stage without interrupting or discontinuing the recognition of mind essence. Think of the sun as being the completion stage and its automatic sunlight being the development stage. When the sun shines, it need not chase after what it shines upon: it simply continues to shine. If the sun had to run after every ray of sunlight in all different directions, it would be impossible for it to continue shining.

As long as the sun does not move away from itself, the light naturally and spontaneously projects. When the recognition of mind essence is lost, it is like losing the sun itself. How can there be any sunshine without a sun? If the dharmakaya is lost, how can there be a sambhogakaya? Without dharmakaya and sambhogakaya, how can there be the unobstructed capacity of nirmanakaya? That disappears as well. If the empty essence and cognizant nature are lost, the capacity is confined. The unconfined capacity becomes limited conceptual thinking. The state that results is unaware, oblivious; we sit not knowing anything.

Unifying the development and completion stages is only possible through truly understanding the threefold principle of essence, nature and capacity. When they are seen as indivisible, then the unity of development stage and completion stage is possible. Otherwise, it is not. To reiterate, the relationship between emptiness and cognizance is like the sun shining. It is not necessary to fuse the sun with its sunlight, and there cannot be sunlight without the sun shining. Likewise, the development stage as the unobstructed expression of nondual awareness cannot exist without a recognition of the essence itself.

Without recognition of the essence, your attention chases after its expression and becomes caught up in it. This is exactly what happens to all ignorant sentient beings. It is like the sun chasing after its light. To use the previous metaphor, we fail to acknowledge the space as it is. We fail to recognize that the sun is shining. We continuously become caught up in the reflection of the sun in pools of water. That is how ordinary thinking is, being caught up in and chasing one reflection after another.

PURITY

THE MOST BASIC PRINCIPLE of the innermost Vajrayana teachings is the indivisible unity of primordial purity and spontaneous presence. Spontaneous presence, the perceiving quality, cannot possibly be separated from the state of primordial purity, emptiness. Do not think of these as two separate entities. Because of the accommodating empty quality of primordial purity, experiences can take place, just as a rainbow can only appear within space and not anywhere else. The key point here is indivisibility, unity. Nothing is perceived separate from the perceiving empty wakefulness.

The five elements and the five aggregates only appear in these forms due to our delusion and ignorant fixation. In ultimate truth, there is nothing other than empty cognizance, which is indivisible. The perceived, the experiential contents that are usually called "appearances," are in actuality never separate from empty cognizance. It is taught that our experience appears as the five elements and five aggregates only because we ignorantly fixated on and solidified the five-colored lights that are the natural radiance of the original ground.

We fixate on manifestations — the elements of earth, water, fire, wind and space — as truly existing, when in fact they are a "nonexistent presence," a presence that appears but which does not possess a self-nature. Awareness itself is empty wakefulness that is primordially pure. The five elements are in reality the five female buddhas and the five aggregates are the five male buddhas. Within their pure nature, they are all simply a display of original wakefulness, indivisible empty cognizance. Space and wakefulness are inseparable. They are primordially a unity.

Primordial purity is the empty quality of this original wakefulness. Spontaneous presence is the manifest, awake quality. Original wakefulness is the indivisibility of these two aspects, the indivisibility of perceiving and being empty. So, we cannot say that one aspect is the cognizance, and that it is separate from another aspect that is not. In fact, deities are depicted in union in order to symbolize this indivisible unity. The female deity represents the empty quality while the male deity signifies the cognizant quality. Their union represents the indivisibility of emptiness and cognizance.

If the male and female deities are indivisible, then both must have the essence endowed with the five wisdoms, right? It is not that the male has the five wisdoms and the female does not. It is taught that the natural purity of the five elements is the five female buddhas, while the natural purity of the five aggregates is the five male buddhas. This means that everything is primordially pure. It is not like something happens through meditation practice and suddenly everything becomes pure. The five elements and the five aggregates are primordially pure as the mandala of the male and female buddhas. This is known as the "all-encompassing purity of whatever appears and exists." In this context, what "appears" refers to the five elements, while what "exists" to the five aggregates.

In other words, the content of experience is the five female buddhas, while that which experiences them are the five male buddhas. So, how can there be any impurity anywhere? Impurity is temporary. If impurity were primordial, it would be impossible to be purified, to become a buddha.

Because delusion is temporary, it can be purified. The sky is primordially pure and unchanging, while the clouds in it are merely temporary. Understand the difference between space and clouds: the primordially pure essence is like space, while the temporary obscurations are like clouds. Since all the impure aspects, such as the five aggregates, the five elements, the five disturbing emotions and so forth, already have the nature of primordial purity; it is possible to purify them. When you churn milk, you get butter, don't you? That is the meaning of "everything is all-encompassing purity." If you churn water, will you get butter? In this sense, everything is like milk: whatever appears and exists is all-encompassing purity. This is exactly why, through recognizing this purity; we can be enlightened.

The training in this basic state of things involves the development, recitation and completion stages. This training helps you develop the notion of how things are; it helps you recognize that everything primordially is all-encompassing purity. Through such practice you will eventually mature: your body matures into the deity; your voice matures into mantra; your mind matures into samadhi. So, first you receive the teachings on deity, mantra and samadhi. This is the same as getting the idea, "If I churn this milk, butter will appear." Then, you "churn and churn," meaning you "train and train" until you have actualized deity, mantra and samadhi. Finally, everything is seen as Samantabhadra. You *are* Samantabhadra: it's all the same butter.

Everything that appears and exists is from the very outset all-encompassing purity. To recognize this is the starting-point of inner Vajrayana. However, this is not the case with the Hinayana tradition, or even the Mahayana. In Kriya, the first of the outer tantras, the practitioners are on the verge of understanding this point. In Upa and Yoga, they are approaching quite close, but are still not truly there. In the case of outer Vajrayana, the view of purity is more like an assumption, imagining that a deity exists beyond what the practitioners experience. They imagine that by making offerings and invoking the deity; it will emerge from somewhere and bestow blessings. It's rather like thinking: "I am right here, an ordinary person. The deity, superior to me like a king, descends from the sky above and I ask him to bestow the siddhis." This is the general approach in Kriya, Upa and Yoga practice. Mahayoga involves a different approach: pointing out that everything, whatever appears and exists, is already all-encompassing purity. What appears and exists, the elements and aggregates, are already the mandala of the victorious ones. In Anu Yoga, you think, "This body is the mandala of the victorious ones." In Ati Yoga, mind is the mandala of the victorious ones, and the three vajras are complete within our experience. That is how the different levels of teachings are distinguished.

To repeat: all that appears and exists are primordially the male and female buddhas, the all-encompassing, pure mandala of the victorious ones. It's much more important to recognize this than to merely sit and read aloud lines of liturgy. Of course, a sadhana practice is adapted to samsaric mind in that there are different attributes to which we can relate. For instance, the deities are depicted with human-like qualities with different body colors, living in a big beautiful house. After having invited them from that "other place," we give them something to eat and tell them how nice they are, just like we do with guests. This all seems very tangible and comprehensible, doesn't it? However, the heart of sadhana practice is not these social niceties. It is the understanding of basic purity.

To practice the development stage in its truest sense, you must let your visualization unfold out of the expanse of the three kayas and conclude by dissolving everything back into this expanse. Otherwise, there is no authentic beginning or end. As I mentioned previously, you begin with the samadhi of suchness, which is great emptiness. To correctly practice this, you need to recognize the natural state of emptiness. Now, this is something that *is* possible; you do not need to imagine or fabricate it. In the Sarma system, you say the *shunyata* mantra and tell yourself, "Everything becomes emptiness," and then you imagine it. From this emptiness the dark blue triangular mandala of space usually appears, followed by those of earth, water, etc. Finally, atop the summit of Mount Sumeru is the celestial palace with four sides and four gates, and so on and so forth. This is how the normal development stage is carried out. But truly, without recognizing the natural state of emptiness, the dharmakaya, no real or authentic development stage can take place.

To allow the real development stage to manifest, we need to dissolve everything into emptiness and then let the mandala manifest from within that state. We must identify the deity at the beginning, meaning at the time of the empowerment. Since the deity is essentially nondual awareness, the awakened state, without recognizing such awareness there is no real deity to train in and to subsequently realize. So, to train in the authentic development stage there is no way around having the nature of mind pointing out. The exercise in *imagining* a deity is merely thought activity, which can never become the real deity.

From within that state of emptiness, let compassion emerge; then, within indivisible emptiness and compassion, the seed-syllable appears. Without that unity of emptiness and compassion, it is impossible to practice the real development stage.

To only imagine the sadhana is labor, mere construction work. It's like building a temple: first there is the mud, then you build up the walls with stones. If you fabricate it in this way, it's not really the abode of a deity; it's merely another human dwelling-place. Deities are not composed of flesh and blood; they are visible emptiness. The abode of the deity should be the mandala of the five elements, with Mount Sumeru, the vajra cross and the celestial palace. It is literally an immeasurable palace in that it is beyond dimensions. If the deity had a form of flesh and blood, you could build a concrete palace and invite the deity to move in. You could say, "Samantabhadra, please sit down here. Dinner is on its way!"

The purpose of training in the development stage is to deal with the normal, samsaric, frame of mind that sees two-ness where there is no duality of subject and object, no separation of the outer perceived object and the inner perceiving mind. We grasp the nondual as dual. In actuality, it is indivisible. Can you separate heat from flame, or wetness from water, or sweetness from sugar? In the same way, you cannot separate the perceiver from the perceived. Unity means "not two, but one." In the realization of pure oneness, how can there be a hell and someone being reborn there? If there is duality, on the other hand, then there is a place and someone taking rebirth.

What we should recognize is the state of nondual emptiness and cognizance. Pure awareness is not an object to be recognized just as we are not a subject recognizing it. As long as duality is constantly re-made, as long as it does not become oneness, there is no enlightenment. But do not apprehend a "oneness" either. Duality should become oneness, and this oneness should be objectless, traceless. It is not a thing we must keep up or maintain in meditation, because there are not two things; there is not subject and object. There is simply oneness. He's Samantabhadra, I'm Samantabhadra.

By acknowledging this basic state of things, all that appears and exists has become all-encompassing purity. But to say "has become" is not right either because it hasn't "become," it has always been. By failing to recognize this one point, you are missing something vital, something essential. Doing this is called "knowing 100, but lacking one." We may be expert in 100 topics; yet, by failing to recognize the nature of our mind, we can still end up in the three lower realms. Unless you know the natural state of mind, you cannot avoid the possibility of going to the three lower realms; you have not eliminated the potential for a low rebirth. Another saying goes, "As long as you don't know the key point of mind, whatever you do is upside down." As long as you are unaware of the nature of mind, what is the way to liberation? What other method is there for liberation, apart from knowing the nature of mind? If you do not know this key point of mind essence, then whatever you do misses the main point. It doesn't matter how successful you might be in worldly terms. On the other hand, if a porter carries his load while recognizing mind essence, he will become an enlightened porter without doing anything else whatsoever. If a porter knows mind essence and trains in that he will transcend the three realms of samsara at the very same time he is plodding along with his burden. Once he can fly in the sky, then nobody will be able to put a load on his back. This is truly so if you practice the pith instructions; it is amazing.

On the other hand, imagine that the king of the whole world dies, leaving behind an ordinary, stinking corpse. He roams about in the bardo utterly powerless: whatever he accomplished, whatever he acquired, whatever he conquered during his life amounts to nothing. His life was an exercise in total futility: he got nothing whatsoever out of it. Now, how is that in comparison with the porter who practices until he is able to fly?

The point is that you will not reach enlightenment by accumulating money, power and prestige. If this were the case, poor people would never be able to reach enlightenment. That's not true at all! Instead, the Buddha said, "Be poor. Stay in solitude for the rest of your life, and die all alone in a cave."

These days the Dharma has turned completely upside down. That's why so few people become enlightened. Instead of remaining poor and not worrying about security and comfort, everyone focuses on getting rich. Once they're rich, they become the slaves of their possessions, guarding them all day and having a difficult time sleeping at night because they're worried their belongings might disappear. That's where the self-deception slipped in. The Buddha himself did not own a house. He slept in the forest under a rock overhang, or under the trees.

The Buddha himself was extremely poor. If you look at what material things he possessed in his life, he had only his Dharma robes, a begging bowl, and a strainer to use as a filter when collecting water. The begging bowl was used every day in begging for food. Whatever happened to be put into your begging bowl was what you ate that day. Sometimes a family would only offer seven peas in the bowl and the monk would have to be content with those. So, the Buddha was extremely poor even among poor people.

The Buddha never said, "Accumulate wealth." The Buddha was very kind in that he didn't discriminate: rich and poor people have equal opportunities to become enlightened. It is due to the kindness of the Buddha that beggars can become enlightened. Unfortunately, rich people usually do not. The old Kadampa masters said, "Entrust yourself to the Dharma; entrust the Dharma to poverty; entrust poverty to living in a cave until death."

ACCOMPLISHMENT

THERE ARE TWO TYPES OF REALITY. One is the truth as it seems to be for most people, while the other truth is how it really is. The first type, how things seem to be for many people, is called the shared karmic phenomena of the same species. This means things look as they do for those who have the karma to be born as a particular class of sentient being. Concerning how it really is, though, everything is no more than a seeming presence, an apparent mental event. Look closely, and ultimately there is no arising and nothing really taking place. Nevertheless, superficially or relatively it does seem as though something happens.

When a yogi reaches perfection in practice by reaching the stage known as the "exhaustion of all phenomena," all ordinary appearances vanish. Deluded experience simply subsides: in his or her experience, deluded phenomenon as seen by other beings ceases to be. That does not mean it vanishes for those other people. Of course if all beings attained enlightenment it would cease; but unfortunately this is merely theoretical. The general experience of sentient beings does not fall apart very easily, whereas the individual deluded experience of a practitioner can diminish and disappear. When all sentient beings are enlightened, their shared deluded experience also vanishes.

Do not expect that your deluded experience will cease because we have a glimpse of nondual awareness. Experience is unceasing; what dissolves in that moment is simply our fixation on the appearance of things. The more this inner fixation dissolves, the more our inner feeling of solidity vanishes, until finally it becomes as Götsangpa Gönpo Dorje sang, as included in the *Rain of Wisdom:*

Appearances are an insubstantial play.
All the relative forms of this magical trickery
Are wide open and penetrable,
Like the rock behind my back.

At that point, he leaned back onto the solid rock and made an exact imprint of his head and back. Milarepa could fly and move freely through solid rock. It is not that such yogis are miracle-workers: they have simply realized the original nature of things as insubstantial. This becomes increasingly evident as the inner fixation on solidity is allowed to dissolve. The more we train in the awakened state, in letting go of fixation, the more the outer world will be seen as it really is — an insubstantial play of illusions. That is why the great masters who attained accomplishment could walk on water, pass through solid rock and remain unharmed by flames. Padmashambhava was burned at the stake several times, but remained unscorched. The outer elements are only deluded perceptions. No one else created them but us; thus, when our inner fixation caves in, their falsehood also collapses. "All appearances are insubstantial like smoke and mist." Superficially they do appear, but only as the magical play of delusion.

At this point, I would like to tell some of the many stories about incredibly accomplished masters who by the power of their realization defied the experience of ordinary people. Milarepa once took shelter from the rain inside a yak horn. He did not shrink himself, nor did he enlarge the yak horn; nevertheless, he could sit comfortably inside the horn. He called out to his disciple Rechungpa and said, "Son, come in and sit with your father. I'm taking the narrow part and leaving most of the space for you. Please come in." Rechungpa could not even get his hand inside. If you visit the Jokhang in Lhasa and look above the main entrance to the temple, you will see this very same yak's horn mounted up under the roof.

When someone attains accomplishment, feats like these are possible: in fact, they are not a problem at all. In the innermost recesses of the Asura Cave at Pharping in the Kathmandu Valley is a tunnel that connects this cave to the Yangleshö Cave down below, about half a mile away. It is not a big hole. Wind passes through this passage and you can feel the draft when sitting near it. Although Padmasambhava could traverse freely through solid matter, he used this narrow tunnel to move between Yangleshö Cave and the upper Asura Cave. When we were restoring the cave a few years ago, the caretaker discovered that hole out through which the wind blew. He said, "Padmashambhava is supposed to have traveled through this tunnel, but it's so narrow that only a rat or an insect could get through it. Maybe Padmasambhava was that size!"

Another example of great accomplishment was Longchen Rabjam. Longchen Rabjam was called a "sky yogi," as opposed to a "water yogi" or "earth yogi" or "wind yogi." Sky yogi means that his realization knew no limits in any direction. It was immeasurable, totally inexpressible, beyond analysis or concepts. It is impossible to measure the realization of Longchenpa. To really fathom the unfathomable wisdom mind of Long-chen Rabjam, you would have to be someone like Jigmey Lingpa, or at least like *his* two chief disciples, the mahasiddhas Tra Drubchen and Do Drubchen. "Drubchen" means mahasiddha. Or, at the very least, you would have to be like their main disciples who lived in the last century during the time of Jamyang Khyentse Wangpo, Jamgön Kongtrül, Chokgyur Lingpa, and Paltrül Rinpoche.

Longchenpa's full name was Samantabhadra Appearing in Human Form, the Victorious Sky-Yogi Longchen Rabjam. Longchen Rabjam literally means "all-encompassing vast expanse." In the term "sky-yogi," "space" means no center, no edge and no end. Space is not produced by causes and conditions; it has no beginning, no present and no end. "Yogi" literally means "connecting with the real," in the sense of taking to heart and making it real in one's experience.

If you want to know more about Longchenpa's realization, you must read his *Seven Treasuries* that were all like tantras in themselves. They arose from the indestructible vajra sphere in the center of his heart through his indestructible vajra throat and onto his indestructible vajra tongue. Because of this, his words are indeed indestructible vajra words. When Jigmey Lingpa stayed in strict retreat at Samye Chimphu for three years and three fortnights, he had three consecutive visions of Longchen Rabjam. During these visions, he received from Longchenpa the complete Hearing Lineage, or oral transmission.

When Longchenpa passed away, the earth quaked six times in a row and there were six great claps of thunder. He passed away in the manner called "rainbow body with remainder," as opposed to rainbow body without remainder. Rainbow body with remainder is more beneficial for other beings, because it leaves behind relics. Among his remains, his brain became one large relic. It was a particular type of relic, called *shariram,* that was one unbroken piece, white in color, with a design on it in a slightly yellowish hue resembling ivory. When great lamas visited the district of Lhodrak where the relic was kept, they would request a segment of it. Taking a hammer and chisel, they would chip off a piece. Within a year, the missing piece would be regenerated and the brain would resume its original form as a single intact relic.

At Tsurphu, a piece of this relic was kept in the "treasure-chest of sacraments." My monastery at Dzong-go Ling had a piece of this relic abut the size of a finger-joint. However, at a certain point, the Tibetan government sealed up the treasure-chest and prohibited people from chipping off pieces of Longchenpa's brain. Then the Chinese came and destroyed the temple where it was kept, so it was probably lost or destroyed. I have not yet heard of anyone having saved or hidden it. Thus, even his physical body was still able to benefit beings for a very long time.

Longchen Rabjam was a contemporary of the Third Karmapa, Rangjung Dorje. They had the same teacher, the great Dzogchen vidyadhara known as Kumararaja. Therefore, the Karmapa Rangjung Dorje held the lineages of both Mahamudra and the Great Perfection. Because they had the same teacher, Longchen Rabjam and Rangjung Dorje were thus Dharma brothers. Despite this equal status, Longchen Rabjam received clarification from Rangjung Dorje on many points regarding clearing hindrances and bringing forth enhancement.

One dawn, while Rangjung Dorje was staying in strict retreat in a tiny hut under a cliff overhang above his main seat in Kham, called Karma

Gön, Vimalamitra appeared in wisdom-body, which is a form composed of rainbow light. He dissolved into the spot between Rangjung Dorje's eyebrows. Afterwards, Rangjung Dorje wrote down what is today called the *Karma Nyingtig* or the Karmapa's Heart Essence, which is a complete system of Dzogchen teachings. Rangjung Dorje was known as a Mahamudra master, but in actuality he practiced both Mahamudra and Dzogchen.

The same was true of Milarepa, who once sang, "I will now sing for you the story of how I went crazy. First Tilo Sherab Sangpo, Prajnabhadra, went crazy. Then, after him, Naropa, the Great Pandita, went crazy. After him, the Great Translator, Marpa, went crazy. Now, I, Milarepa, am crazy, too! The vicious, demonic influence of the teachings of the Middle Way has made me crazy from the front. The insane teachings of Mahamudra have made me crazy from behind. The demon of the Great Perfection in my heart has made me totally mad! That's how I happen to be crazy now." Actually, not just Milarepa, but most masters have practiced both Mahamudra and Dzogchen.

In the Kagyü Lineage, it is said that the "cubs of the snow lioness are often more eminent than their mother." Frequently disciples become greater in influence than their masters. Milarepa's disciple, Gampopa, had many, many students. Among them were three principle disciples. One, Seltong Shogom of Nangchen, was quite extraordinary, and his disciples were remarkable as well. They could fly through the sky. When the sun rose in the morning, they would fly to the opposite side of the valley to catch the rays of the sun. Wherever they set off from or landed, the whole flock, guru and disciples alike, often left their footprints in the rock.

Once my father took me to see the footprints and I counted more than 30 sets all in a row. In those days they obviously did not wear shoes, because all the imprints were of bare feet. One could see the imprints of the heel and toes very clearly. When the afternoon sun was sinking, the flock would fly back to the opposite side of the valley to catch its last rays and warmth, and again they would leave similar footprints.

When Seltong Shogom passed away, the dakinis took his body and enshrined it within a stupa in a cave. The cave was located 15 stories above the ground, with no road or path leading to it. No one could reach the cave. Inside the cave, was a stupa with the "sacred word" design, which was made of sand. Later on, the King of Nangchen raised story after story of tiny ladders up the cliff wall, so that finally people could reach the cave and see the stupa. Over the centuries, people offered applications of gold-leaf out of respect, so that eventually the whole stupa appeared to be made of pure gold. This is not a mere legend from the distant past: I myself went and saw these signs. Since all of Seltong Shogom's disciples were simultaneously liberated and left this world, no one remained to continue the lineage: it died out right then.

The same is true of the early masters of both the Drikung and the Drukpa Kagyü lineages. The masters and their disciples, and then their disciples again, were increasingly more eminent, like the saying about the cubs and the lioness. Disciples can indeed be more illustrious than their masters.

Here is another story about rainbow body. During the days of Khyentse and Kongtrül, there was a person who obtained rainbow body who became quite famous. He was called Nyag-la Pema Düdül, and this event was witnessed by many people. I personally know of two people who left this life in rainbow form. One was a Vajrayana lay practitioner in the region of Derge. The other person took rainbow body in the cow shed of one of my gurus" mother's household. This event was witnessed by several people. Jamgön Kongtrül the Second told me this story, so I definitely feel it is true. Jamgön Kongtrül's brother, a very tall and handsome man, was present at the time.

It happened like this. An elderly nun came through their village on pilgrimage. When she saw the wealthy household she asked for a place where she could make a short retreat. They offered her one of their vacant cow sheds. She told them, "I want to use it for a week to make a strict retreat. I want the door sealed up. Please pile stones against the door because I don't want any disturbance." Since they were used to sponsoring practitioners, they agreed and no one thought twice about it. They said, "Sure, you can have it your way." They didn't know who was going to look after her and bring her food; they thought she had already made arrangements.

After three days, some strange phenomena began to occur. Scintillating, swirling light-rays of different colors were seeping out of the holes and cracks of the cow shed's stone wall. Light was shining out from under the roof; while outside the shed, spheres of light moved rapidly about. The people of the house wondered, "What's going on here? Who's looking after the old woman? Who's bringing her food?" They asked their servants. The servants thought someone else was giving her food, but actually no one was. They decided she must have been cooking for herself, but Jamgön Kongtrül's brother asked, "Is there any place to cook inside?" The servants said, "No, no. There is no fireplace or anything." So they wondered, "What is she eating? Does she have any water? What are these lights all about?"

Finally, they decided to take a look. They removed the pile of stones and pried open the door; they saw that the body of the nun had fallen to pieces. Her hands were lying in one place and her feet were lying in another; her limbs were no longer connected to the body, but lay scattered in pieces. From the ends of the bones, swirls of rainbow light were coiling out as the body continued to fall apart. The observers asked each other, "What is this? It looks like she's dead!" One person had the presence of mind to say, "Let's leave her alone. It looks like something unusual is happening here. She asked for seven days of solitude so let's do as she asked." And saying that, they sealed the shed up again.

When they returned after the seventh day and opened the shed, the rainbow lights had vanished. Not a drop of blood, nor flesh, nor bones could be found anywhere. Only the nails from the fingers and toes remained, lying there very neatly, along with a hank of hair. This event most definitely happened.

Even after the Chinese arrived, two or three people in Golok attained rainbow body. Nyoshul Khen Rinpoche, who is very careful about such stories, went to Tibet and through many different sources tracked down the names and places of these people. He is keeping all the details very precisely. Two of these people attained rainbow body. The third person was being beaten by the Chinese when suddenly he started to levitate upwards until they could not reach him. He went higher and higher until he vanished. This is a type of celestial accomplishment. So, it's definitely true that even these days people do attain rainbow body, and that there are still practitioners who attain accomplishment.

The terma tradition gives direct teachings on how to attain rainbow body. In the Kagyü tradition, it is said that mind dissolves into dharmata, while the body dissolves into atoms. Of the 84 mahasiddhas of India, not a single one died leaving a corpse behind. Of Padmasambhava's 25 disciples, only one person left a physical body behind at the time of death. His name was Langchen Palgyi Senge and his body is still enshrined in a stupa at Paro Taktsang.

In the present age, it seems as though people are not very diligent. They do not apply themselves continuously to the teachings; they do not practice day and night. This is the only difference between the present situation and that of the past, when there were so many great practitioners. The teachings themselves are still available through an unbroken lineage; they have not disappeared.

Here is another interesting story about a practitioner who attained a high degree of accomplishment. I heard this from my uncle, who never lied to me, so I feel it is definitely true. This incident took place in the encampment of the great mahasiddha Shakya Shri, in Central Tibet. My uncle Tersey Tulku, who was one of his close disciples, was staying with him then. One day a lama from Kham walked in, with an attendant carrying his baggage. Now, this attendant that walked straight into the center of the camp was a corpse, a dead body. When the lama shouted "Phat!" the corpse fell to the ground. The lama took his luggage off the corpse, got out whatever he needed, and set about cooking himself dinner under the open sky.

Later, my uncle heard the lama tell how this situation occurred. The lama said, "I came from Kham, and this is the corpse of my benefactor.

After death he became a zombie. Now I'm taking his corpse to dispose of at Sitavana, the Cool Grove Charnel Ground, one of the major sacred places in India. Since the zombie can walk, I thought it might as well carry my things. But don't let anyone near it or disturb it in any way. Just leave the corpse alone."

Of course, no one could be kept away. Everyone wanted to see the corpse who carried the lama's luggage. The corpse was as dried out as a stick, and because it had no shoes, all the skin and flesh of the feet had worn off. Only the bones were visible. No one could quite believe it. Anyway, the next morning the lama woke up, loaded his bags on the back of the corpse and shouted "Phat!" The corpse stood straight up and started to walk, slowly, placing one foot rigidly in front of the other. It could not walk very fast, so the lama went on ahead. He said he always had to keep within sight of the corpse, though, otherwise it would lose its way. If he climbed to the top of a mountain, he would have to wait there until the corpse finally reached him. Then the lama would continue on down the mountain and wait below for the zombie to arrive.

A year later, the lama came back through the encampment. He said that the zombie had walked all the way to Sitavana, where it was cremated. The lama left his sponsor's remains behind, and had to carry his things back to Tibet himself. Tersey Tulku later said he was never really sure whether this lama was playing a big joke or not. Who could be sure if there was really a mind in that dead body? Once you reach a certain stage of stability in rigpa, you can move material objects around at will; maybe the lama was playing a joke on everyone. Still, even if that was the case, it was quite a remarkable joke. The lama was definitely an accomplished master of some kind, and it is a true story.

There is one dangerous thing about real zombies. If the zombie touches you on your head, you become a zombie as well. That's why the lama had to be careful to keep the zombie in sight all the time. If my uncle, who was also one of my gurus, had not witnessed this event with his own eyes, I certainly would not have believed it. But he did witness it. Many strange people visited the encampment of Shakya Shri, the Lord of Siddhas. He was always surrounded by 700 meditating disciples. One of the strangest visitors was this lama with the zombie.

Many realized masters have clairvoyant powers or super-perception, as illustrated by the Karmapas. Our present minds are covered up by conceptual thoughts. When those are absent, it is possible to know the minds of others. The reason is thoughts move in the same basic nature. What is thought by one person can appear in another's mind, like an image reflected in a mirror. A mirror does not have to make any effort for an image to be reflected in it; it occurs naturally. In the same way, a buddha sees all three times and directions simultaneously, effortlessly and vividly. My teacher Samten Gyatso was like that. He would often speak out what other people were thinking. Many people did not dare to go in his presence for precisely that reason, because when he uttered what they were thinking, they became scared. Think of it this way: when the sky is clear, there are not two skies; it's only one. That is how the yogi's mind is unimpeded.

Khakyab Dorje, the 15th Karmapa, was an outstandingly great master, incredibly learned and very accomplished. He had unimpeded clairvoyance and was probably one of the greatest masters of his time. However, he did not have complete control over his clairvoyance. For example, he would know when some lamas would die and where they would be reborn, without being asked for this information by anyone. Often he would have already written out the circumstances of the tulku's next rebirth when the searchers would come to inquire. With other lamas, though, the Karmapa could only see the circumstances of rebirth when a special request was made on the part of the Sangha and some auspicious circumstance was thus created. With other lamas, he could not see anything, even when requested for help; he would say, "It's shrouded in mist." This, he said, would be due to some problem between the deceased lama and his disciples. If there was fighting and disharmony among a lama and his followers, the whereabouts of his next incarnation would be indistinct, as if they were obscured by haze. The Karmapa said, "The worst obstacle for recognizing tulkus clearly is disharmony between the guru and disciples."

In such cases, there would be nothing to do: the circumstances of the next rebirth would remain invisible.

Another incredible master who had unimpeded clairvoyance was Jamyang Khyentse Wangpo. Tashi Özer, the great khenpo of Palpung monastery in Eastern Tibet, said he once met Khyentse Wangpo who said, "Oh Khenpo, what trouble you have! From morning until night, you have to do all these different things." He started mentioning all the different things the Khenpo had to do. He knew everything, every little detail. "You are really bothered by all these things; you have no free time at all." Khyentse Wangpo knew how busy Tashi Özer was, day and night. Then he said, "All these people down in the village, they are so full of disturbing emotions. They have so many problems, don't they?" Then Tashi Özer would have to say "Yes, that's true, Rinpoche" even though he didn't have that kind of clairvoyance, because if you made any objections to what he said, Khyentse Wangpo would get angry, annoyed. You had to say "Yes, Rinpoche."

One day when Tashi Özer was there, Khyentse Wangpo suddenly cried out, "Oh no, what has happened, it's terrible!" They asked him what was wrong. He said "Far away at such-and-such place, there is a bald monk who fell over the side of the cliff. While he was falling, he shouted out "Khyentse Wangpo, Khyentse Wangpo." I heard it, and then while I was thinking about it, somehow he became stuck in the branches of a tree. Now the other monks are trying to pull him up with ropes. Yes, now they've gotten him up. That's what alarmed me." The next morning a bald-headed monk came to visit Jamyang Khyentse. He said," Oh, last evening I had a strange accident," and told the whole story. He explained how he was walking with a stick and a load and fell over the side of the cliff, at which point he shouted out "Khyentse Wangpo! Khyentse Wangpo!" He didn't fall all the way down, but became caught in some branches, and was then pulled up with a rope. Khyentse was amazing. His activity was unceasing and after he died, Dzongsar Khyentse appeared, who was equally amazing. Then when Dzongsar Khyentse set, Dilgo Khyentse rose.

BARDO

ALL SENTIENT BEINGS ARE IN A SITUATION called *bardo*. Bardo means an intermediate state which is between two points of time. Right now we are in the intermediate state between our birth and our death called the *bardo of this life*. This bardo lasts from the moment we take birth until we enter the circumstances that will cause our passing away. Two other bardos are sometimes included within the bardo of this life. They are called the *bardo of meditation* and the *bardo of dreaming*. We need to train in the bardo of meditation during the daytime and the bardo of dreaming during the night. Now, to train in the bardo of meditation, we need to understand what is meant by buddha nature.

Buddha nature is present in everyone, without any exception. It is the very core of our being, the very nature of our mind. It is nature totally free from all faults and fully endowed with all perfect qualities. What we need to do now is simply to recognize our nature, and then sustain the recognition of that. There is no need to create or manufacture a buddha nature through meditation. It's also essential to realize that every experience manifests and vanishes within the expanse of our buddha nature.

The bardo of meditation takes place during the period of time we are able to recognize our buddha nature, the dharmakaya nature of our mind. Involvement in conceptual thinking is not called meditation. Meditation in this context refers to the time when the thought has ceased and there is an absence of conceptual thinking. To repeat that period over and over again, from the cessation of thought to its re-occurrence, is called training in the bardo of meditation. Unless we recognize this nature, we will continue in samsaric existence, taking rebirth in one realm after the other.

Sentient beings take birth from one place to the next in samsaric existence precisely because of not recognizing their nature. This lack of knowing their nature is called ignorance.

Essential meditation teachings are called pith instructions, and they are both profound and direct. To illustrate this point I will tell about pith instructions given by Paltrül Rinpoche. Once, Chokgyur Lingpa went to a tent camp in the province of Golok to meet Paltrül Rinpoche, and stayed with him a week. During that week Chokgyur Lingpa and his daughter received transmission for the *Bodhicharya Avatara* and essential meditation teachings.

One evening Paltrül Rinpoche taught the daughter of Chokgyur Lingpa, Könchok Paldrön, who was to become my grandmother. She remembered his words very clearly, and later repeated them to me. She imitated Paltrül Rinpoche's thick Golok accent, and said, "Don't entertain thoughts about what has passed, don't anticipate or plan what will happen in the future. Leave your present wakefulness unaltered, utterly free and open. Aside from that, there is nothing else whatsoever to do!" What he meant was, don't sit and think about what has happened in the past, and don't speculate on what will appear in the future, or even a few moments from now. Leave your present wakefulness, which is the buddha nature of self-existing wakefulness, totally unmodified. Do not try to correct or alter anything. Leave it free, as it naturally is, free and wide-open like space. There is nothing more to do besides that. These are the vajra words of Paltrül Rinpoche, and they are truly meaningful.

Present ordinary mind is that quality or capacity that is conscious in everyone, from the Buddha Samantabhadra and Vajradhara all the way down to the tiniest insect. All sentient beings are aware or conscious. That which is aware or conscious is what we call mind, that which knows. It is conscious, yet it also is empty, not made out of anything whatsoever. These two qualities, being conscious and empty, are indivisible. The essence is empty; the nature is cognizant; they are impossible to separate, just as wetness can't be separated from water, nor heat from a flame.

Once this nature has been recognized, training in the bardo of meditation can begin. At the moment of not recollecting anything from the past, not being involved in contemplating the future and not being pre-occupied with something else in the present; let your present wakeful-ness gently recognize itself. When you allow this, there is an immediate and vividly awake moment. Do not try to modify or improve upon this moment of present wakefulness. Leave it open and free as it is.

As for the bardo of dreaming, dreams only occur after we have fallen asleep, don't they? Without sleep, there are no dreams. What we experi-ence while dreaming is experienced due to confusion. After we awaken, from where did the dream come? Where has the dream experience gone? We cannot find either of those places. It's exactly the same with the delu-sory daytime experiences of all the six classes of beings.

Examine where your dreams originate from, where they dwell, and where they disappear to. Understand that although the dream does not truly exist, we are still deluded by it. Now, consider the dream as an exam-ple for our being conditioned by ignorance. The buddhas and bodhisat-tvas are like people who have never fallen asleep and therefore are not dreaming, while sentient beings, due to their ignorance, have fallen asleep and are dreaming. Buddhas exist in the primordial state of enlightenment, a state that is completely undeluded. This state moreover is endowed with all qualities and free from all defects. Cut through your day-time confu-sion, and the double delusion of dreaming atop deluded samsaric exis-tence ceases as well.

After the bardo of this life comes the *bardo of dying*. The bardo of dying begins the moment we catch an incurable disease that will cause our death, until the moment we draw our last breath. The period lasting from the inception of illness until our spirit leaves the body is called the bardo of dying.

It is said that the best possible achievement is to be liberated into the expanse of dharmakaya during the bardo of dying. If we have recognized our basic nature of self-existing wakefulness and grown accustomed to it through repeated training; a supreme opportunity arises at the moment just before physical death. If we are adept enough we can engage in *dhar-*

makaya phowa, the mingling of self-existing awareness, the dharmakaya nature of mind, with the openness of basic space. This is the highest kind of phowa: in it there is no ejector and no thing to eject. You remain in utterly pure samadhi; mind indivisible from basic space. Dharmakaya is like space in that it is all-pervading and impartial. When nondual awareness mingles with basic space, this all-pervasiveness and space are inseparable. The foundation for dharmakaya phowa is the realization of the self-existing wisdom that is present in each one of us. It is our awareness that needs to be recognized. Mingle awareness with the clear sky and rest in the phowa where nothing is moved, ejected or transferred. This liberation into primordial purity is the foremost type of phowa.

If you have not recognized nondual awareness, or have not trained sufficiently, and therefore can't effect dharmakaya phowa, the bardo of dying will progress further. The "outer breath" of perceptible inhalation and exhalation will cease, while the "inner breath" of subtle energies still continues to circulate. Between the ceasing of the outer and inner breaths occur three experiences called *appearance, increase,* and *attainment.* These take place when the white element from your father, situated at the top of the central channel at the crown your head, begins to move downwards, inducing an experience of whiteness that is likened to moonlight. Next the red element from your mother, situated below the navel, begins to move upwards to the heart center, generating an experience of redness that is like sunlight. The meeting of these two elements brings about an experience of blackness followed by unconsciousness.

Simultaneous with the unfolding of these three experiences, all the different "80 innate thought states" arising from the three poisons of desire, anger and delusion cease. There are 40 thought states that arise from desire, 33 thought states that arise from anger and seven thought states that arise from delusion. Every one of these ceases at the moment of blackness. It is like the earth and sky merging: everything suddenly grows dark. The conceptual frame of mind is temporarily suspended. If you are a practitioner who is familiar with the awakened state of nonconceptual awareness, you will not black out and fall unconscious at this point. Instead, you will recognize the unceasing and unobstructed state of rigpa.

To reiterate, first there is the whiteness of *appearance,* second the redness of *increase* and finally the blackness of *attainment.* These three are followed by the state called the *ground luminosity of full attainment,* which is the dharmakaya itself. People who are unfamiliar with the awakened state of mind revealed by the cessation of conceptual thought will at this point revert into a state of oblivion — the pure and undiluted state of ignorance that is the very basis for further samsaric existence.

For most beings, this oblivious state of ignorance lasts until the "sun rises on the third day." However, an individual who has received instructions from a spiritual teacher and has been introduced to the true nature can recognize dharmakaya and attain enlightenment at this point, without falling into unconsciousness.

This recognition and awakening are often called the merging of the luminosity of ground and path, or the merging of the luminosity of mother and child. Through the power of genuine training in the bardo of meditation this recognition occurs as naturally and instinctively as a child jumping onto his mother's lap: the mother and the child know one another, so there is no doubt, no hesitation. This recognition occurs instantaneously. A tantra declares: "In one moment, the difference is made. In one moment, complete enlightenment is attained." If this happens, there is no reason to undergo any further bardo experiences. Liberation is attained right then.

For someone who fails to be liberated at the moment of death, according to the *Liberation Through Hearing in the Bardo* known among Tibetans as *Bardo Tödröl,* the ensuing bardo states are said to generally last 49 days, with a certain sequence of events occurring every seven days. This is true for the average person who has engaged in a mixture of good and evil deeds. For a person who has committed a great deal of evil during his lifetime, the bardo can be very short; he or she may plunge immediately into the lower realms. For very advanced practitioners the bardo is also very short, because there is immediate liberation. But for the ordinary person who is somewhere in between these two states, the intermediate state is said to last an average of 49 days.

After the bardo of dying the *bardo of dharmata* begins. Ordinary people feel they have woken up after being in an unconscious state for three and a half days; to them it seems as though the sky unfolds again. Various dissolution stages occur during the bardo of dharmata: mind dissolving into space, space into luminosity, luminosity into unity, unity in wisdom and, finally, wisdom dissolving into spontaneous presence. Here, this unity refers to the form of the deities. First, colors, lights and sounds will occur. Only four colors appear at this time, and this is called the experience of the *four wisdoms combined*. The green light of all-accomplishing wisdom is missing at this point, because the path has not yet been perfected. "Luminosity dissolving into unity" refers to the forms of the deities. Different deities begin to appear, first in their peaceful and then in their wrathful form. Some are as tiny as mustard seeds, while others are as big as Mount Sumeru. The most important thing at this point is to recognize that everything, whatever appears, is a manifestation of your nature. The deities are your own manifestations: they do not come from anywhere else. So, feel 100% confident that whatever is experienced is nothing other than yourself. Another way of explaining this is that whatever appears is emptiness, and that which experiences is also emptiness. Emptiness cannot harm emptiness, so there is no point whatsoever in being afraid. With that kind of confidence, it is possible to attain liberation at the sambhogakaya level.

The light from the peaceful and wrathful deities is intense and overwhelming. If you have received instructions regarding this stage, you can recognize them with confidence as expressions of your own essential nature. Otherwise, pale, soft lights representing the six realms will appear in different colors. Those who are unfamiliar with such phenomena will be naturally attracted to those more comfortable types of light, and this attraction is what pulls the mind back into the six realms of existence. In this way the fourth bardo, the *bardo of becoming,* begins.

During the bardo of becoming, your power of perception is seven times clearer than during the normal waking state in this life. You will remember whatever you have done in the past and will be able to understand whatever is taking place. You will possess six recollections: the ability to remember the teacher, the teachings, the yidam deity for whom you have received empowerment, and so on. When remembering the teachings you received and practiced, it is most important to acknowledge that you have died and are in the bardo state. Next, try to remember that everything that takes place in the bardo is deluded experience. While various things are perceived, they lack any self-nature, unlike in our present experience. Now, if we put our hand into boiling water or into a flaming furnace it will burn. Likewise, we can be crushed by the weight of huge stones. But in the bardo, nothing that takes place is real. Everything is just an illusory experience — so how can it harm you? This is very important to keep in mind.

At this point in the bardo, the force of your intention is unobstructed. It is thus possible to take rebirth in one of the five natural nirmanakaya realms, the five pure lands of the nirmanakaya buddhas. The easiest place to be born is in Sukhavati, the Blissful Realm of Buddha Amitabha. Buddha Amitabha made thirteen eminent vows in the past, and due to the strength of these it is not necessary to have purified all disturbing emotions before being reborn in his pure realm. To enter the other buddhafields, total purification is necessary, but this is not true for Sukhavati. What is most important here is to be free from doubt. Engendering one-pointed determination like an eagle soaring through the sky, think without any hesitation, "I will now go directly to the pure land of Amitabha!" If you can hold to this single thought in the bardo of becoming, that alone is sufficient to go there. As long as you are not attached to anything, nothing can tie you down or prevent you from reaching Sukhavati. To be sure that you are free of attachments, before death, mentally offer everything you own to Buddha Amitabha. Make a mandala offering out of all your possessions and enjoyments, relatives and friends. Anything to which you remain attached, even something as small as a needle and thread; is enough to act as an anchor for your mind.

When the body is left behind, only the consciousness continues on — all alone like a strand of hair plucked from a slab of butter. If the consciousness is not bound by attachment to anything in this world, then nothing can hold it back, though the existence of doubt can make some difference. A consciousness that harbors doubt about rebirth in the pure land of Amitabha can still be reborn there, but it will remain captive inside a closed lotus bud for 500 years, until it has purified the obscuration of doubt. If you can surrender all attachment to the things you have known in this life and one-pointedly make the resolve, "I will go straight to Amitabha's pure land," then it is 100% certain that you will arrive. There is no hesitation or question whatsoever about this.

In the bardo of becoming you will remember, "My stability in practice was not sufficient for me to be liberated into dharmakaya at the moment of passing away. It was also not quite sufficient to be liberated into sambhogakaya during the bardo of dharmata. So now here I am in the bardo of becoming." Acknowledging this, make up your mind to be completely free of attachment to anything. Otherwise, even the smallest attachment to relatives or possessions will obsess and worry your spirit, like a dog chasing a scrap of meat. Only such attachments can really tie your consciousness back to this world.

If you do have to be reborn in this world, you will continue through the bardo of becoming while seeking a new rebirth. When meeting the parents who will give birth to you, imagine them as the yidam deity with consort. Let your mind enter the womb in the form of the syllable HUNG, and make the resolve to become a pure Dharma practitioner.

The Vajrayana teachings provide many opportunities, many chances on different levels. If we miss one opportunity, we get another chance, and if we miss that there is still a chance to try again. As long as your samayas are unbroken, there are many precious teachings in Vajrayana that will help you cross the bardos.

When you are fatally sick or when you face death, make up your mind to combine the practice of recognizing mind essence with the resolve to go straight to the pure land of Sukhavati. As the great master Karma

Chagmey said, "May I soar like a vulture in the sky directly to Sukhavati, without looking back for a single moment!" Don't look back! Remain totally unattached to anything in this world. Don't have any doubt: then there is no question that you will go straight there.

Always remember to begin with taking refuge and forming the bodhichitta resolve to benefit all beings. For the main part of practice, imagine yourself as the yidam deity. This is called the development stage. Gently look into, "Who is it that visualizes? What is it that imagines all this?" Not finding anything which visualizes or imagines is called the completion stage. At the very same moment of looking into the thinker, the fact that there is no thing to see is immediately seen. Anyone can see that, if they know how to look. In the very first instant there is an absence of thought. This state is not like a black-out, in that you are not unconscious, but vividly awake. Yet this wakefulness doesn't form thoughts about anything. It's like space; not the night sky, covered by darkness, but like the sky lit by sunlight, where the sunlight and space are indivisible. That is the naked ordinary mind present in everyone. It's naked because at that moment there is no conceptualizing, no thought activity. Ordinarily, every moment of consciousness is occupied with conceptualizing and creating something. Therefore, leave your present wakefulness totally unfabricated.

Remember always to conclude your practice by dedicating the merit and making pure aspirations. The pain may be very strong when we are seriously ill; we might be in agony and feel miserable. Give up the thought, "I'm suffering! How terrible it is for me!" Instead, think, "May I take away all the pain and sickness of all sentient beings, and may their stream of negative karmic ripening be interrupted! May it all be taken upon myself! May I take upon myself all the sickness, difficulties and obstacles which the great upholders of the Buddhadharma experience. May their hindrances ripen upon me so that they all are free from any difficulties whatsoever!" Such an attitude accumulates an immense amount of merit and purifies immeasurable obscurations. It is difficult to find anything that can create more merit than keeping this perspective. It is much, much better than lying there moaning, "Why should this happen to me! Why do I have to suffer?" That kind of self-pity is not of much use.

The wishes we make when we are close to drawing our last breath are incredibly powerful. It is said that the resolve the mind forms at the verge of death will definitely be fulfilled, whether it is pure or evil. Some people die with the thought, "So and so did that to me! May I take revenge!" Through the immense strength the mind displays during the last moments before expiring, that person's mind can be reborn as a powerful evil spirit with the ability to harm others. On the other hand, if we make pure wishes and aspirations, there is no question that they will be fulfilled. With the finality of our human life acutely on our minds, the wishes we make and resolves we form are immensely powerful. This is very important to remember.

At the moment of death, "time does not change, experiences change." Time here means that there is no *real* death that occurs, because our innate nature is beyond time. It is only our experiences that change. All these experiences should be regarded as nothing but a paper tiger. When we meet a real tiger, we will feel frightened, but if we see that it is merely an imitation — a paper tiger — we are not frightened at all. We have no fear that the paper tiger will eat us. In the same way, all the different experiences that occur after death all seem real, yet they're not. In the bardo, flames cannot burn us, weapons cannot cut us; everything is illusory and insubstantial. It is emptiness.

At Tulku Chökyi Nyima Rinpoche's monastery, called Bong Gompa, north of Central Tibet, the bursar was about to pass away. My uncle, Tersey Tulku was present. While the bursar was dying, he never stopped talking. He said, "Well, well, now this element is dissolving, now that element is dissolving, now consciousness is dissolving into space. Now space is split open and all the different manifestations are appearing. The vajra chains are fluttering around like crystal garlands and fresh flowers. Dharmata is truly amazing!" He was laughing, and then he died. Of course, he was someone who was quite stable in awareness.

The experiences that will appear at death and after are inconceivable, and cannot exactly be described beforehand. One thing is certain, however: whatever is experienced is a "mere appearance without any self-nature," merely felt to be, yet insubstantial. Everything is the play of emptiness. Whatever is experienced is nothing other than a manifestation of your innate nature — visible, but with no concrete substance.

Not recognizing that whatever appears in the bardo is your nature; you can be terrified by the sounds, frightened by the rays and afraid of the colors. These sounds, colors and lights are the natural manifestation of buddha nature. They are, in fact, the Body, Speech and Mind of the enlightened state: the colors are the Body, the sounds are the Speech, and the light rays are the manifestation of Mind. They appear to everyone, without exception, because everyone has buddha nature.

Although these experiences appear to everyone, they can differ in the length of time they are experienced. This probably corresponds to the degree of stability in mind essence. Other than this difference in duration, the experiences are the same for everyone. The most important thing to remember is not to feel sad or depressed about anything — there is no point in that. Instead, have the attitude of a traveler who is returning home while joyfully carrying the burden of the suffering of all sentient beings.

CONDUCT

OF THE TWO ASPECTS OF VIEW AND CONDUCT, it's said that we should "ascend with the conduct" — start with the conduct at the bottom and work up. This means first study and practice the teachings of the shravakas; next the teachings of the bodhisattvas, and finally those of the Vajrayana. Start with the bottom and work up — ascend with the conduct. We do this first by contemplating the four mind-changings, then practicing the specific preliminaries, then doing yidam practice, and finally ending with the three great views. The three great views are known as Mahamudra, the Great Seal; Dzogchen, the Great Perfection; and Madhyamika, the Great Middle Way.

As I mentioned earlier, the Buddha described his teachings in this way:

Just like the steps of a staircase,
You should train step-by-step
And endeavor in my profound teachings.
Without jumping the steps, proceed gradually to the end.

Just as a small child
Gradually develops its body and strength,
Dharma is in that same way,
From the steps of entering in the beginning
Up until the complete perfection.

Accordingly, we should behave in conformity with the basic teachings, starting from the bottom, just as we would on a staircase. We cannot climb a staircase by starting at the top; we must begin with the first step.

The view, on the other hand, should be unfolded from above: that's why the saying continues "while descending with the view." Imagine a canopy or parasol that is unfolded above oneself: the view should descend from above in this way.

We must be careful because there is a way of perverting this basic principle and turning it completely upside down, so that one ascends with the view and descends with the conduct. This means to behave according to the highest vehicle while holding a view that starts from the bottom. This is called perverting the teachings. We should get the highest view, but behave first like a shravaka, then like a pratyekabuddha and slowly like a bodhisattva. Regarding conduct, start from the bottom; not the other way around. You will not find any teaching anywhere that says, "Keep the view of a shravaka, or an even lower view, while acting like a Dzogchen yogi." This is a very important principle: keep the view as high as possible, but behave with a very low profile. Act like a shravaka, then a pratyekabuddha, then a bodhisattva. This is called unfolding the view from above, while ascending with the conduct from below.

The view of Mahamudra, Dzogchen and Madhyamika is identical in essence. Although it is said, "The ground is Mahamudra, the path is the Middle Way, and the fruition is the Great Perfection," in the view itself there is no difference whatsoever. In my tradition we do not select only one particular view among these three. The naked, natural state of mind does not exclusively belong to any specific category of Middle Way, Mahamudra or Dzogchen. These three are taught here as one identical nature. The awakened state of Mahamudra doesn't differ from the awakened state of Dzogchen or Madhyamika. Buddhahood is the final fruition of all these regardless of which of these paths you follow, just as when you approach the Vajra Seat in Bodhgaya from north, south or west, you arrive at exactly that spot. It does not matter from which direction we approach it; the ultimate destination is the same.

To be a real yogi, someone who truly realizes these three great views, first recognize the natural state of awareness. Then, train to develop the strength of that recognition by sustaining its continuity. Finally, gain some degree of stability. That is the only authentic way. Some people, though, want this to happen on the spot. They do not want to undergo any of the preliminary practices, nor subject themselves to the yidam-training that is known as the "main part" of the practice. Some people want nothing but the view. That would be fine if it really was enough, but it isn't.

The main reason why you cannot only teach the view is that quite a few people will then miss the main point by believing, "I only need the view! There is nothing to do! I can give up all activities!" Of course, this may be true in some sense; however, what happens when someone gives up conventional Dharma practice too early is that such a person fails to do any spiritual practice in terms of purifying obscurations and gathering the accumulations. At the same time, he or she does not truly realize, progress in, and attain stability in the view. The end result is that the view remains an idea while your behavior shows no regard for good and evil. That is what Padmasambhava meant by "losing the conduct in the view."

We need to integrate view and conduct. Padmasambhava said as well, "Though your view is higher than the sky, keep your deeds finer than barley flour." Understand the expression "finer than barley flour" to mean to adopt what is virtuous and avoid what is evil, with respect for the law of cause and effect, with attention to the smallest detail. This is to keep harmony between view and conduct. The opposite, separating one's actions from the view, is to somehow convince oneself that there is no need to do the preliminary practices; no need for any good deeds; no need for making offerings and no need to apologize for evil actions. One can fool oneself into believing one need only remain in simplicity. What this honestly means, though, is that such a person will have no spiritual progress. Ultimately, it is definitely true that there *is* nothing to do, but this is true only after one has passed through to the other side of understanding, experience, and realization. To maintain an intellectual conviction of the view without having undergone the training is a severe misunderstanding. This is how the self-professed "Dzogchen practitioner" goes astray.

In Tibet many people committed this grave error. Westerners cannot really be blamed for this fault yet, since the Dharma is only now taking hold in their countries; the understanding of practice is just being established. Tibet, on the other hand, was a country where the Dharma had been taught and understood for many centuries. Yet many people went astray in this fashion, not simply a few. Frankly speaking, there may have been more people in Tibet with a "make-believe view" than with genuine insight.

I do not feel I can really blame Westerners who heard stories about the Buddha and the Indian siddhas receiving the teachings on mind essence and nondoing, and who then think, "Well, we are the same, there is nothing to do. Everything is fine as it is."

It is honestly not such a simple matter to arrive at the correct view. You must connect with a true master; you must have the necessary intelligence. Then you must go all the way through the training. It is much easier to glare at benefactors with wide-open eyes and look about with an air of Dzogchen. Most people behaving like that are actually charlatans. Often they could not help it; without some dishonesty it could be hard to get by and gather donations. Playing the simple meditator and keeping a low profile would not be successful — who would know about your realization then? If you happened to be an upstart lama with a penchant for fame and fortune you would have to brag a little. You needed to tell about how many Dharma lineages and teachings you held, how long you stayed in retreats, how special your realization is, how you tamed both gods and demons, and the like. Then things would happen; you would be swarmed by sponsors and followers like a piece of rotting meat covered with flies. Yes, honestly, there were more fake lamas in Tibet than authentic ones.

Some people have the habit of thinking that something is bound to happen after practicing meditation a while — like going through school — that after ten or fifteen years you end up with a degree. That's the idea in the back of people's minds: "I can make it happen! I can *do* enlightenment!" Not in this case, though. You cannot make enlightenment, because enlightenment is unconstructed. Realizing the awakened state is a matter of being diligent in allowing nondual awareness to regain its natural stability. It is difficult to reach enlightenment without such diligence, without undertaking any hardship.

Faced with the reality of not progressing in the so-called "meditation practice" of a conceptually constructed view, you might get discouraged: "I can't get enlightened! I spent three years in retreat and nothing has happened!" On the other hand, if you practice in an authentic fashion you will definitely become enlightened; there is no question about this. Training assiduously with devotion, compassion and loving kindness while repeatedly letting be in unconstructed equanimity, you will surely discover the true signs of spiritual practice. These signs are the acute feeling that life is impermanent and that there is no time to waste; that the Dharma is unfailing; that there is genuine benefit from training in samadhi; and that it is truly possible to overcome conceptual thinking.

While these are taught to be the most wonderful signs of progress, a materialistic type of person will not see them as being so wonderful. He wants a flabbergasting meditation experience. If something astounding happens that he can see or hear or maybe even touch, he thinks, "Wow! I am really getting somewhere now! This is completely different from what I am used to — such a beautiful experience! Such bliss! Such clarity! Such emptiness! I feel totally transformed! This must really be *it*!" [Rinpoche chuckles.]

On the other hand, when you reach the "even plains" of nonthought, the simple quiet after conceptual thinking dissolves, there is nothing very exceptional to see or hear or grasp. You may feel, "Does this really lead anywhere? There is nothing special in this!" Honestly, the view is not something spectacular; on the contrary, it is free from pinpointing anything particular at all. The person who doesn't comprehend this fact will think, "What's the use of this? I worked so hard for years, and nothing is really happening! Maybe it would be better to visualize some deity. Maybe I should chant some special mantra which would give me powers, and then I could show some results of practice, some real accomplishment!" People do fall prey to this type of thinking.

During this process, your subtle disturbing emotions remain intact; eventually they manifest again and take over your being. Why wouldn't they? Everyone is overcome by disturbing emotions unless they are stable in nondual awareness. Only the moment of the awakened state does not become caught up in deluded emotion. Nondual awareness is the most effective way, but the materialistic practitioner does not appreciate this. He wants an altered state, a special experience, an extraordinary dream. When it happens he congratulates himself, "Excellent! This is the real thing!" Such is the weakness of human nature.

My root guru Samten Gyatso once said, "I have not had a single special experience. As the years pass by, my trust in the authenticity of the Dharma grows. I am confident in the truth of the three kayas. From the age of eight I looked into the essence of mind, and since then I have never forsaken it. My diligence varied and of course I became distracted at times, but mostly I have kept to the practice of mind essence." I only heard him say this once; otherwise he would never discuss such personal matters.

At the same time Samten Gyatso was so intelligent and learned, so attentive to every little detail, so skilled in every little task, so steady and trustworthy, that people would regard him as being like Marpa the Translator. Samten Gyatso was so precise in all matters that if you got his word on something you would never later hear him say that he forgot. That's the kind of man he was, extremely dependable, totally reliable.

His eyes burned with an astonishing brilliance, like the flame of a butter lamp at its end, somewhat like the bright eyes of a kitten. Coming into his presence, it felt as if he was penetrating your innermost core, laying bare your innermost secrets. Anyway, he was scrupulously attentive to all his daily affairs, both spiritual and secular. He never postured or put on the air of high realization. In Tibet there was no shortage of people of *that* kind — people who never lowered their vacant, glaring gaze to the ground, and who spouted random statements like "All the phenomena of samsara and nirvana are great equality!" [Rinpoche laughs.] Actually, what do you gain from such pretense!

So you see, it is possible to lose the conduct in the view. It is also possible to lose the view in the conduct. Caring for others, helping them with medicine and education, is definitely virtuous. However it must be done out of an attitude of the four immeasurables, without any selfish aims for fame and respect, and without dwelling on the idea "I am doing good! I am kind to others!" To act out of the four immeasurables involves creates virtuous karma of the general conditioned kind. Helping others out of a pure selfless motivation is the best form of conditioned virtue; it is truly wonderful!

Unconditioned virtue, on the other hand, is the training in thoughtfree wakefulness. Many people ask, "How does sitting in meditation practice help others? It would be much better to go out and give them food and medical care and build them schools." People may have the attitude of wanting to act for the welfare of others before having accomplished anything him- or herself. Helping others is definitely virtuous, and it does help them somewhat. You of course create good karma by helping others, but such altruistic action does not necessarily mean you will be liberated. Only after liberation can you immeasurably benefit all beings.

The most important technique for avoiding pitfalls on the path is knowledge and trust in the Dharma. Knowledge means comprehension of what is and what is not true, through studying and understanding the teachings. The real knowledge, however, that which we should really be diligent in, is understanding the view. View, meditation, conduct and fruition all depend on the view. Diligence in meditation involves the development stage, while diligence in conduct refers to the bodhisattva trainings.

A very important factor is an unchanging trust in the Three Jewels. You can gain it by considering this: without the Precious Buddha, wouldn't this world be totally blind? How could anyone reach liberation from samsara or the omniscient state of enlightenment? It is solely through studying and following his flawless words, the Precious Dharma, that our congenitally blind eyes will open. Without someone to uphold and transmit these teachings through the spoken and written word, the teachings would surely have died out. The Buddha would have appeared and taught and then nothing; the whole process would not have taken even a hundred years. That we still have the Buddha's teachings available today is thanks to the Precious Sangha, consisting mainly of the great bodhisattvas on the ten bhumis, the sons of the victorious ones, and the arhats. My role is to be teaching the Dharma, and regardless of whether it is pretense or not, I definitely have received the blessings of the Precious Sangha. When I think about it, the kindness of the Three Jewels is absolutely incredible! So how can I help having trust in them?

Knowledge, the other factor, is what helps us to distinguish between what is and what is not true. In ancient times, the Buddha taught that there were 360 religions and belief-systems prevalent in the world. These were also called the "360 wrong views" because they were incorrect, consisting mainly of different varieties of eternalism and nihilism. The true view was taught by the Buddha. There is a simple reason for this: a sentient being cannot realize the correct view that is unmixed with concepts, because the mind of any sentient being is conceptual. The only way to transcend conceptual mind is to follow the words of a fully awakened one, a buddha.

Knowledge is what distinguishes between truth and untruth, between what is correct meditation training and what is not. As we gradually progress through deeper levels of learning, as our knowledge broadens, our fixation automatically diminishes. Isn't fixation and clinging the root of samsara? When there is no more clinging to painful or pleasant situations, we are free from samsara. As Tilopa said, "You are not bound by what you experience, but by your clinging to it. So cut through your clinging, Naropa!"

It is also said, "The sign of learning is to be gentle and disciplined." Imagine a piece of paper burned in the fire — it becomes totally soft. A sense of peace is the true sign of learnedness. "The sign of meditation training is a decrease in disturbing emotions," meaning that the training of looking into mind essence dissolves your three or five poisons, which is the unrecognized expression of your essence. This occurs the moment you recognize it. The disturbing emotions vanish without a trace, like flames extinguished.

Sentient beings chase around after all sorts of myriad things. Now is the time to take a rest. Otherwise, we will continue to roam around in samsaric existence. Nothing other than mindfulness can really block off or halt your karma. It is our karmic actions and disturbing emotions that force us to wander through samsara, and it is these karmic actions and disturbing emotions that we need to relinquish. Don't we need to stop being under their control? Isn't it true that the moment of the view does not lie subject to karma and disturbing emotions? The view is the real reason why the buddhas are not under the power of karma and disturbing emotions; they have captured the stronghold of the view.

Realizing the view, authentically and totally, melts away the obscurations of karma and disturbing emotions, and this allows the qualities of original wakefulness to unfold. This is the real meaning of "buddha," The awakened state of mind. If you could truly allow this to happen, wouldn't that then be the absence of all defects and perfection of all virtues? The correct view is what clears away all faults. Stability in the view reveals the essential nature of mind free of obscurations, like the sky that cannot be dyed any color or to which nothing can adhere. Yet the sky itself is not something that can vanish. Please understand this vital point!

Short moments, many times. That is how to train, because in the beginning, the genuine recognition of our innate state doesn't last very long. Some people say, "I have meditated a lot! I was in retreat for one year! Believe me; I did a three-year retreat." There is a tendency to think that a three-year retreat is a flabbergasting feat. Honestly, how do three years compare with beginningless samsara? It is nothing more than a speck of dust!

Someone may inflate their chest and conceitedly proclaim, "I did it! I meditated for a full three years!" During my early years in Nepal there was an elderly man who often told people, "I actually have done slightly better than the Buddha. He stayed six years practicing on the banks of the Nairanjana river, but I have done nine years of retreat!" [Rinpoche chuckles.)

It is often said that to plan to practice some time in the future is to let obstacles slip in before the practice even begins. Most people let the time slide by, thinking, "I really want to practice the Dharma more and I will surely do so later on in my life!" Other people may believe that the time has come to act for the welfare of others, while in fact they do not possess the qualifications to effectively do so. They think, "Now I will teach! I can really help others! I can make a difference!" Then they run about in the world pretending to work for sentient beings.

Generally speaking, Westerners are quite sharp when it comes to comprehending the natural state. If they would also practice it afterwards! And not only the natural state: we need to train ourselves to exert effort in virtuous actions. Engaging in evil requires no effort at all; it is spontaneous. Killing others, stealing their possessions, lying and so forth requires almost no effort at all. One need not teach insects how to kill each other. No sentient being needs training in the three negative karmic actions of the body carried out on the physical plane; we engage in them quite spontaneously. Even animals needn't be taught how to kill.

Without having to study, we know quite naturally how to carry out the four negative actions of speech: lying, using harsh words, slandering, and engaging in idle gossip. No one needs to train in the three negative actions of mind: ill-will, craving, and holding wrong ideas. We all seem to know quite well how to carry out these activities. Sentient beings are already experts; it happens quite spontaneously due to the ripening of past karma. Dharma, on the other hand, is something we need to study.

To roll a big boulder up to the top of a mountain we need to push it all the way up. But to let it roll down into the valley, we need not do much; we let go and it rolls down all by itself. Nudge a stone and it will roll downhill all by itself, but there is no such thing as a stone that rolls uphill. In the same way, we do not need to study how to engage in negative actions. Sometimes, when giving in to the impetus to carry out a negative action we are under the power of karma. At other times we feel faith in the teachings; we feel good-hearted, compassionate and devout and so forth, yet this is very rare. That is why it is said, "Those who don't practice are as abundant as the stars at night; those who do practice are as scarce as morning stars." This is due to karma.

For those with good karma, the situation is different. A great Kagyü master sang, "Even in my mother's womb, my spiritual aspirations were awakened and I had the desire to practice. At the age of eight, I remained in equanimity." That's an example of good karma ripening.

Again, although you may have a very high view, you should still keep a refined level of training. Here, refined means that you pay close attention to and remember impermanence and your mortality. When you reach the point of not being distracted from the recognition of mind essence, impermanence is not such an important issue. If something is impermanent, let it be impermanent; if it is not, then it is not. Only when you have no distraction whatsoever does one not need to think about impermanence.

"High view" in this case means to pay close attention to how things are, such as impermanence. "Good meditation" does not only mean being skilled in the development stage or yogic exercises; it means facing the fact that everything is impermanent. It also means to reach the point of nondistraction. In other words, one does not sleep at night; one does not fall into the delusory dream state, but is able to recognize dreams as dreams. During deep sleep, there is a continuous long stretch of luminous wakefulness. When one reaches this point, there is no need to dwell on impermanence anymore.

The Tibetan word for enlightenment is *jangchub,* which means "purified perfection," or in Sanskrit, *bodhi.* Literally, this means the complete purification of the two obscurations, along with habitual tendencies; and the perfection of all qualities of wisdom. It is like a lotus bud that, having grown out of the mud, fully blooms. Until this occurs, we should practice as the masters of the past advise: "Go to a retreat place, either in a forest or in the mountains. In a remote, quiet spot, take a comfortable seat, supplicate your guru one-pointedly, and inspire yourself by thinking of impermanence with compassion."

In Kham, there is a saying, "When you want to boil water, you can blow on the flames or pump the bellows, as long as the water boils." In the same way, if all the different practices we do benefit our stream-of-being, then that's fine. If you can remain in nondual awareness without meditating and without being distracted, everything is fine. But if your nondual awareness is merely imagined, or if you try to construct it in meditation, it will remain merely a concept. If awareness becomes carried away, then you are in delusion. The key word here is undistracted nonmeditation. When nondual awareness is totally free of confusion and distraction, then your water has really boiled.